W.H. Auden, Poetry, and Me

A 102-year-old reluctant poet reflects on

life, poetry, and her famous teacher

by Debbi Shannon

with Gladys Dubovsky

I have made every effort to trace the owners of copyright material and secure permission. I apologize if any person or source has been overlooked.

Published in the United States of America.

Book cover design by Robin Locke Monda
http://www.robinlockemonda.com/

Book interior design by David Provolo
https://reedsy.com/david-provolo

Photograph by Sharona Jacobs
http://www.sharonaphoto.com/

Second edition

Published by Fogbow Books, LLC, New York.
www.fogbowbooks.com

Gladys and I met for brunch every Sunday for years. We talked about current events, politics, books, family, relationships, life, death, and whatever we thought might be beyond death. At times, she quoted poems that she had written through the years.

"I took W.H. Auden's poetry class at The New School, and it changed my life."

At 102, it's safe to say that she has seen and done everything, and yet, this class was the most important thing that has ever happened to her. I knew there was a story there.

"He was an incredibly lovely man," she said.

"May I ask you about the time you spent with Auden? I'd like to write your story, if that's all right."

"Sure, but I don't think it will be all that interesting. Who would want to read my story?"

I smiled. "You might be surprised."

Gladys kept track of Auden throughout the years. While listening to her stories and researching Auden's life, I saw many similarities in their life experiences. Something else happened that was unexpected: I fell in love with W.H. Auden, the poet and the man, just as Gladys had done.

Some say that our lives are like threads in an infinite tapestry that twist, separate, run parallel, and at times, come back together again. I hope you enjoy reading Gladys's stories as much as I have enjoyed listening to her tell them, then writing them down.

I want to thank Gladys for trusting me and for her patience, advice, wisdom, kindness, friendship, and love. Gladys, if I may borrow your words—there is no here without you.

— Debbie Shannon

Me, Gladys Dubovsky, in school, aged 8

Chapter One

The class I took with W.H. Auden at The New School in New York City in the winter of 1940 was the best thing that has ever happened to me—and that's saying a lot considering that I'm 102 years old. To tell you the truth, I never dreamed that I would live this long, but here I am. And all these years later, that one class and the time I spent with that extraordinary man still affects me. It's as fresh in my mind today as the day I stepped into the class.

Meeting Auden changed me in a way that nothing else has. I've led a pretty extraordinary life so far. I've loved deeply, cultivated great friendships, experienced incredible joy and sorrow. I've had my fair share of ups and downs, but who hasn't? It's been an incredible ride.

Both my mother's and father's families came to New York City from Russia. Well before WWII, pogroms in Russia were large-scale, targeted, and frequent. A pogrom is an organized, violent attack against a particular ethnic group, most notably Jews, with the intent of massacring, persecuting, and purging entire populations from a town or village. The word pogrom comes from a Russian word meaning "To destroy, to wreak havoc, to demolish violently."[1] These brutal pogroms in Russia happened all the time, and they were devastating.

Peasants and city folk secretly organized these riots, raided a Jewish village, and proceeded to loot stores, destroy homes, rape the women, and execute the men. A typical pogrom lasted for days.[2]

The military frequently forced thousands of men and boys to enlist in the army and sent them far away with little or no warning. The Russian military under Tsar Nicholas II sent a notice to my father, Abraham Tarshis, saying that he had to report to the recruiting office that week to enlist. Papa was just fourteen years old and knew that the chances of getting out of the army alive were next to nothing. If he went, he would most certainly die.

Papa knew of a family named Levy who were leaving Moscow to live in London. I hesitate to assume that my grandparents made the arrangements, because even though Papa was just fourteen, children were very independent back then. They had to be in order to survive. Whichever way the arrangement came about, the Levys agreed to falsify their travel documents stating that Papa and his younger brother, whose name I don't know, were their own sons. That's how our ancient surname went from being Tarshis to Levy. Papa had always wanted to change his name back and die a Tarshis, but he never got around to doing it.

London was very polluted at the time, and my uncle, who was asthmatic, found it hard to breathe. After a few years, Papa took him to South Africa where the climate was better. Not long after that, the two of them emigrated to New Zealand. That's where Papa met his first wife and had a son named Harry. As far as I know, I still have family in New Zealand.

Shortly after Papa's son was born, his wife died. I never knew exactly what happened to her, but rumors swirled in our family that her death was unexpected and mysterious. Whatever the circumstances, immediately after her death, Papa took Harry and settled in New York City.

My mother's family also fled from Russia. My mother, Sonia's, family name was Fried, an Ashkenazic Jewish surname. She came over with her brother, Albert, and four sisters: Rose, Bea, Anna, and another sister whose name I never knew. She died before I was born, and Mama never mentioned her. Her parents came over later. I remember Grandpa spent most of his days studying the Torah although he wasn't a Rabbi or teacher. Mama's family were loving and close-knit, and they all settled near one another in Manhattan.

Papa met Mama in New York City, and they eventually married. I was born Gladys Gitel Levy in the Bronx on August 25, 1915. Harry lived with us. He was six years old when I was born, and despite our age gap, we got along well. He used to buy me books. In fact, my love of books is largely because of Harry, and it's a love affair I've had my entire life. I loved Harry and trusted him. That's what made what happened between us so confusing and painful.

One evening when I was about five or six years old, my parents went out for the evening and asked Harry to babysit me. After my parents left, Harry found me in my room and began to fondle me, and then raped me. Afterwards, he warned me not to say anything to anyone.

"This is a secret," he whispered in the dark. "You can never tell anyone."

Just as Harry had asked, I never said a word to anyone. He never let on that something terrible had happened nor did he act differently around my parents. I watched him sweet talk them, smooth as grease, and they never suspected a thing. Everyone behaved as though nothing ever happened. After that first time, whenever we were left alone in the house, he eventually found where I was hiding and raped me.

I tried telling myself that he wasn't really violating me—that there had to be a reason why he was doing these things to me. For years, I tried to look at things from his point of view. He was a small boy when his mother died. His father moved him to a new country and married a strange new woman who never welcomed him into her home as her son. Finally, they became engrossed by the new baby in the house.

I grappled with the good side of him paying attention to me and giving me books with the bad side who took advantage of me—who knew very well that he was hurting me. I tried to justify his actions, but make no mistake, what he did was wrong and he knew that very well. No matter what happened to him before I came on the scene, that's no excuse for his behavior.

I kept this secret for many years. I only recently told my family. Dan asked me why I never invited Harry around anymore, so I told him. It took a lot for me to talk about it, because saying it out loud made it real.

The abuse continued for three years until I was eight years old. That's when our family moved north from the Bronx to Mohegan Colony. I'm not sure why Harry stopped. He may have found that the newer, smaller house was too risky even for him, or he may have tired of me, but his pattern of psychopathic tendencies continued throughout his life.

Scientists believe that our biological predispositions shape how we react to our environment, and that how we react to our surroundings and experiences shape the structure and organizational features of our brains. A number of factors, such as bad or neglectful parenting, the separation from a parent or lack of parental involvement, genetics, and the child's environment, can contribute to developing psychopathy. How we grow into adulthood might be equal parts genetic and environment.[3]

With regard to Harry's early environment, I know he lost his mother as a boy, and my father was never exactly Ward Cleaver from *Leave it to Beaver*. Those profoundly affected him. When Harry was about seventeen or eighteen, he suddenly left our house and the Colony. I think he became an accountant, so he had to have gone to college although my father would have never paid for him to go. Wherever he went, I was happy not to see or hear from him for many, many years.

Mohegan Colony was a progressive community established in 1924 on the south end of Mohegan Lake in Westchester County, New York by a group of like-minded liberals, socialists, and anarchists. The founders wanted to build a utopian community that provided an egalitarian way of living and raising one's family. There were about 250 families in the Colony. One of the founders, Phil Fried, was my mother's uncle. Our family was more socialist leaning than anarchist, but I prefer to think of us simply as being open-minded.

I was close to my mother, and I accepted my father. The truth is, I didn't like my father. He was a difficult man. He ruled our house with an iron fist. Whatever he said, Mama and I did, and there was no sense in arguing with him. In those days, it wasn't uncommon for husbands to take a more dominant role in running the house—of wearing the pants in the family—but there were times when I felt he deliberately kept Mama and me from doing and having things that brought us joy. Simple things. Our thoughts, opinions, or ideas carried no more substance with my father than a ray of moonlight. Growing up, I never had a bike. We lived in the country, and all my friends had bikes, but he wouldn't let me have one. When I was ten, I wanted to cut my hair and wear it short. My hair was thick and woolly and hot! It never really got long. It just bushed out to the side. Not only did I want to cut it because the bob was all the rage, but a shorter hairstyle would have been cooler and much easier to handle. Nope. He squashed that idea right away. Mama tried to intervene.

"Why can't she cut her hair?" Mama asked him.

"And if she wanted to go out with the boys, you'd let her do that?"

What a ridiculous thing to say about a ten-year-old girl. What was the point of not letting me cut my own hair? Seriously, it was hair for goodness sake. It wasn't as though I asked him to get a tattoo. I just couldn't accept his denial, so I snuck the scissors from his office desk early one morning and cut my hair anyway. Later that day, he caught sight of me playing with my friends. I could just about see the steam rise from his red face when he saw my short hair, but he didn't strike me or shout. In fact, he didn't speak to me for a while, which was fine by me.

When I was older, I wanted to go away to school to study literature. He refused. I was lucky he let me go to NYU to study liberal arts. I'll never understand Papa's stinginess and spite. At times, I felt he was so tormented that if it were possible he would have pulled down the sky just to cover his own misery. Was it because he had to flee his homeland and never saw his parents again? Or maybe he never got over the loss of his first wife? Whatever the underlying reason, Mama and I were prisoners of his misery and there seemed to be no escape.

They say when we die, the memories of the lives we lived are what we leave behind. It reminds me of the poem by Linda Ellis called *The Dash*. On our tombstones, between our birth date and our death date, a dash is carved into the stone which represents the life we lived. In the end, will people say that we made life easier for our fellow man, or did we make things more difficult? Did we love enough? What memories will we leave behind? Right now, how are we spending our dashes?

Chapter Two

I have always loved school. We were taught in the Modern School Movement in the Colony. From 1910 through 1960, anarchists in the United States were establishing a new type of school. The Modern School Movement or the Ferrer School was modeled after the *Escuela Moderna*, which had been instituted in Barcelona and founded by Spanish educator and free-thinker Francesc Ferrer i Guàrdia. The goal of the *Escuela Moderna* was to educate the working class in a non-traditional, non-religious way.[4]

After the Spanish-American War in 1898, Spain was forced to renounce all claim over Cuba, Puerto Rico, Guam, the Philippines, and other islands. After their humiliating defeat, the Spanish wanted to get their political hands on northern Africa. The Spanish government through President Maura, declared war on Morocco, but the people of Morocco unexpectedly fought back. Spain needed additional troops for reinforcements, so it called on the Catalonian reservists to fight. Unfortunately for Spain, these overworked, underpaid people refused to fight for what they saw as the Spanish elites sending them off to their deaths. In trying to force their hand, the Spanish government leaned on the Catalonian people hard. They underestimated the resolve of the Catalans. They staged strikes, riots, and rebellions throughout Barcelona. That defiant week is known as the Tragic Week, or the *Semana Tragica*.[5]

The Spanish government saw Ferrer as a threat because of his progressive views. It accused him, without proof, of fomenting the insurrection, and had him arrested. After a bogus trial, the military court found him guilty. At dawn on October 13, 1909, he was led to the gallows in the trenches of Barcelona's Montjuïc Castle. His execution led to an international outcry—protests broke out throughout Europe and the United States. Many European cities and street were renamed after Ferrer. Statues were erected in his memory.[6]

Although the *Escuela Moderna* closed its doors in 1906, three years before Ferrer was executed for sedition, he inspired anarchists in the United States. More than twenty Modern Schools were established from New York to Los Angeles. In New York City, the Francisco Ferrer Association was created in 1910 by anarchist leaders Emma Goldman, Alexander Berkman, Leonard Abbott, and Harry Kelly. In January 1911, they opened a Modern School located at 6 St. Mark's Place in Greenwich Village. The Modern School of New York, like the *Escuela Moderna* in Barcelona, included a publishing house, an adult education center, and a community center for the city.[7] The school, which had started out with only nine students, grew to become a center for the leftists and labor movements in the city. Margaret Sanger, the American feminist who coined the term "birth control" and whose son, Stuart, attended the school, gave lectures there. Other speakers included writers Jack London, Upton Sinclair, and labor leader and activist Elizabeth Gurley Flynn.[8]

The Modern School was different from the traditional schools of then and now, because the teachers encouraged their students to think for themselves. Students were emboldened to ask questions, think objectively, and become self-reliant. The anarchists not only wanted to establish a new way of teaching, but also to create "a new culture, a new life, a new world."[9]

It's surprising to me that the Modern School Movement remains relatively unknown. Apart from a handful of works on the subject, many people in this country are completely unaware of this extraordinary experiment in education, art, and communal living.

The Stelton Colony in Stelton, NJ was unique in that it was the first of its kind to create an entire living community centered around their Modern School.[10] Harry Kelly, along with my great uncle Phil Fried and others, then founded the Mohegan Colony using the Stelton Colony as a model.

Mohegan Colony was a hotbed of new thinking. I'm very grateful for my Modern School experience, because it taught us to think unconventionally. I remember that for one whole year, our teachers encouraged us to pretend to be pirates. We learned geography and traveled the high seas in our imaginations. We learned how to count doubloons—the golden coins minted in Spain, Mexico, Peru, and Nueva Granada and used by conquistadors. I never really learned math that year, because I could only count doubloons! I learned German when I was ten. Afterwards, I learned French and Latin. Oh, how I loved Latin. And not only that, but even now, it helps with the crossword puzzles. I ended up taking four years of Latin.

A few years ago, I remember watching the movie *Dead Poets Society* and could relate to the scene where Robin William's character, Mr. Keating, jumps up onto his desk.

"Why do I stand up here?" he asked the boys. "I stand upon my desk to remind myself that we must constantly look at things in a different way."

That was the gift that the Modern School gave me—to always look at the world in an entirely new way. Our teachers also taught us to be curious. They never shut us up, and I never lost that ability to think objectively and speak my mind.

That's me with my hand on my best friend, Lydia,
and the rest of the Colony gang

I had six girlfriends in the Colony, and we were voracious readers, devouring anything we could get our hands on. We read *The Well of Loneliness* by Radclyffe Hall in 1928 when we were thirteen. Banned in England until 1959 for violating the *Obscene Publications Act of 1857*, it's a fabulous lesbian coming of age story that has everything: family drama, novel writing, London and Paris in the 1920s, war, romantic intrigue, pathos. After we finished the book, however, we all decided that it might be best if we stopped having sleepovers, because we thought they might cause us to turn into lesbians. Silly girls.

There were only two boys my age in the Colony: one was named Amo, and the other was Manny Vardi. His house in the Colony was not too far from mine. Whenever he went outside to play, it wasn't long before his mother would stick her head out of the window and yell, "Manya, you have to come in and practice!" He became the great Emanuel Vardi, a famous violist. He passed away in 2011 at the age of 95.

When the director of our school in Mohegan felt that his students were ready to progress on to high school, he would call the principal of nearby Peekskill High School and would simply say, "I have three kids," and we were accepted without question.

The rest of the kids at Peekskill, however, shunned us and considered us outcasts because we were different. We consistently ranked highest in all tests and grade scores—just one more reason for them to hate us. The Peekskill kids called us "Free Love" because their parents had taught them to be frightened of anarchists and socialists. Years later, as proof that prejudice was still passed down from one generation to the next, bigotry once again reared its ugly head.

On August 27, 1949, a concert was given in Peekskill featuring such artists as Pete Seeger, Lee Hayes, Woody Guthrie, and the actor/singer Paul Robeson who was the deep bass soloist who famously sang *Ol' Man River* in the musical *Showboat*. The artists were all prominent leftists. On the day of the concert, a mob of five hundred swelled to a thousand or more. The artists and concert goers linked arms and sang *God Bless America*. They tried to defend the concert site, but the crowd lynched Robeson figures in effigy and erected a 12-foot wooden cross on the picnic grounds and set it on fire. They burned books, sheet music, and chairs and danced around the flames. By the time all was said and done, every concert defender had been injured.

Undaunted, the organizers rescheduled the concert for Sunday,

Supporters of Paul Robeson form a defense line
in a field along a road where demonstrators
marched in protest against the concert.
(Permission granted AP Images)

September 4th at 2 p.m. at the abandoned Hollow Brook Country Club. Pete Seeger was to perform as well as several folk singers before Paul Robeson. Pete Seeger came early—at 11 a.m. and found a line of 2,500 union members had formed a human chain to protect the concertgoers from the jeering crowds.[11]

Pete said that he saw about 150 protestors straining against the gate shouting things like "Go back to Russia! Kikes! Nigger-lovers!"

"They were a typical KKK crowd," Pete said, "but without the bedsheets."[12]

The stage was set on a flatbed truck parked under an old oak tree. People gathered around the truck and sat on the grass to hear the musicians play. Even though the atmosphere was tense, there was a general sense that everything was going to go off without a hitch, because they believed that the huge number of police that had gathered would protect them.

After the concert ended at 4 p.m., the police redirected cars and buses leaving the concert to drive up through the steep and winding pathway through the northern Westchester woods. Just around a bend in the narrow road, groups of men and boys stood on either side beside piles of baseball-sized rocks. While holding a beer in one hand and a rock in the other, they unleashed their fury onto the concertgoers. As if on cue, they hurled rocks at the vehicles.

Some men were carrying torches and threatened to set the cars on fire. More than fifty buses and countless cars had their windows smashed. Pete Seeger remembered shouting to a nearby policeman, "Officer, aren't you going to do something?" And all he said was, "Move on! Move on!" One man lost his eyesight. The mob's leaders had been drinking from pocket flasks right up until the moment of the attack.

Fearing the crowd would actually try to lynch Robeson, I was told by friends of mine that they hid Paul Robeson in the safety of the Colony until the riot blew over.

Paul Robeson singing 'Old Man River' at concert in Peekskill.

Photo by Seymour Wally/NY Daily News Archive via Getty Images

*Cars carrying Paul Robeson concert goers
are stoned by demonstrators.*

(Permission granted AP Images)

The violence overflowed to people who weren't even at the concert. Some men and boys noticed a bus of blacks traveling along the highway on their way back from the city and attacked it.[13]

Years later, Pete Seeger spoke with a musician whose father had been a police officer in Peekskill during the time of the riot.

A car from the concert is overturned and smashed.
(Permission granted AP Images)

"You know, that riot was all arranged by the Ku Klux Klan and the police…they had walkie-talkies all through the woods. They had that place surrounded like a battlefield."[14]

After the riots, as a way of singling out those who were in favor of the riots with those who were not, those who participated or agreed with the riots took out subscriptions to the *Star-Ledger* newspaper. They staked delivery boxes on their front lawns. Having that delivery box let everyone know who was who. Those people who didn't have a box on their lawns were not only shunned, but many times attacked—even if they were white. You see, white supremacists aren't only against black people, or brown people, or Jews. They are against anyone who doesn't think the way they do.

All of this reminds me of that song in the musical *South Pacific*—*You've Got to be Carefully Taught*—where hatred and prejudice is carefully taught to the child by his or her parents. It makes me sad, because it's so true. No one is born hating, rather they are taught to hate and fear others who are different. Interestingly, when *South Pacific* went on tour in the 1950s, two Georgia state lawmakers said that anything that justifies marriage between different races was repulsive. One of them, Rep. David C. Jones, wrote, "We in the South are a proud and progressive people. Half-breeds cannot be proud."[15]

Nearly 70 years ago, Oscar Hammerstein wrote about the intolerance of interracial relationships. Not only do we still see those prejudices today, it seems as though we are seeing an uptick in the number of hate crimes committed in this country—at times by Americans against fellow Americans. White supremacists, the KKK, and Neo-Nazis have crawled out of the shadows and have staged violent rallies around the world. A "Unite the Right" demonstration in Charlottesville, VA in August 11-12, 2017 showed masses of white supremacists, Neo-Nazis, and members of the KKK snaking through the night carrying flaming torches. Some of them extended their right arms in a Heil Hitler-style Nazi salute. They gathered to demonstrate against the removal of a statue of General Robert E. Lee, but then why were their chants anti-Semitic? They shouted things like, "Jews will not replace us," "This city is run by Jewish communists and criminal niggers," and "Blood and soil," which is a phrase straight from Nazi ideology which refers to one's ethnic "blood" and their "territory."

The German translation *Blut und Boden* is written on the Nazi

logos. Those thugs came to celebrate slavery and preserve white su-
premacy, and yet, they ranted about Jews and wore T-shirts that had
quotes from Adolf Hitler.[16] Seeing those young men scream that pu-
rulence made one thing horrifyingly clear: we have learned nothing
from history.

Struggle is woven into everything that is right. That's why,
today more than ever, we must continue to strive for peace and
justice for all.

Chapter Three

When I was about thirteen, I was one of those kids who was accepted at Peekskill High School with no questions asked. I wanted to get into the literary society, which was made up entirely from kids from the Colony. In order to be accepted, I had to submit a writing sample. I wrote the following poem called *Blasphemy*. I used the *nom de plume* Gladys Lee at the time, because I liked the way it sounded. This poem got me in:

September 1928

Blasphemy

The dead tree stands
Against the burning sky.
Its blackened arms,
Its twisted, knotty fingers
Clawing at the past.

The creaky laughter,
The rheumatic cowering
In the wind,
Are blasphemy
To the evening sky.

A symbol this?
A skeleton
Of once proud wealth
Left ravaged
By the hungry winds of Time!

And will a breeze,
Stirred to a might wrath
By storm of anguish
Sweep this remaining curse
From the now darkened sky?

When the Peekskill kids weren't shunning us, they were making fun of us. They even made fun of the way we dressed. The Peekskill boys all wore ties, but none of the Colony boys wore ties. In fact, I didn't know of a single boy who owned a tie. The Peekskill girls all wore print dresses, nylon stockings, and heels. We Colony girls wore white shirts, skirts, and Lisle cotton ankle socks with flat, oxford-style shoes that we all got at the Pediform Shoe Company.

For the most part, we kids from the Colony stuck with our own. One morning when I was sixteen years old, I was startled when the girl sitting in back of me tapped me on the shoulder. I turned to face her. She was a very pretty girl with porcelain skin and short, flat, black hair that was as shiny as a bee's wing. As I watched her inspect me, I thought about how nice it would be to have her flat, shiny hair instead of my bushy bird's nest.

"You're from the Colony, aren't you?" she finally asked.

"Yes," I said.

"You look it."

You'd think that was meant to be an insult, but she didn't say it to be mean. The way she smiled at me was anything but threatening. We struck up a conversation and became very close friends. Her name was Lenore Cohn, and her family lived on Lake Mohegan on the other side of the Colony. Before I met Lenore, none of us kids in the Colony had anything to do with the people on the other side of the lake, not because we didn't want to. We just didn't. After that day, Lenore came over to the Colony with a bunch of her friends, and I introduced them to all of my friends.

Everybody smoked back then, and I can tell you the exact moment I started. I was sixteen years old and had a friend named Edna who was a year older than I was. She was very elegant and sophisticated and caught the eye of the boys from the other side of the lake. And she smoked, which made her even more classy to me. One day that summer, she sat down next to me and pulled out a gold cigarette case. She flipped it open and held it out to me, and I took one. I copied the way she held the cigarette between her fingers. She struck a match and held it out for me.

"Now inhale as the flame lights the tip," she said.

I took a long drag as the tobacco at the tip flared orange and crackled. A choke-cough exploded from my lips, and I nearly blew it out. Enda flashed her lipstick-painted smile at me.

"You'll get used to it."

I continued to hack and wheeze, but took another drag, then another as tears streamed down my cheeks. The only thing that ran through my mind as I convulsed and ignored the vile charcoal-burn-taste on my tongue that made me gag was that I was so GLAMOROUS!

Lenore had a boyfriend at the time who came from a famous family. They were very well-known psychiatrists. If memory serves, her boyfriend ended up becoming a psychiatrist as well. They had to keep their relationship a secret, so they met at my house. Apparently, the boy's parents didn't approve of Lenore. It wasn't because she was poor, or Jewish, or any other reason people give to label someone as unacceptable marriage material. I think his parents tried to keep Lenore and her boyfriend apart because they thought the two of them were way too young to be so serious about one another.

One day, two of Lenore's friends, a boy named Matty and his girlfriend Ruth who liked to be called Bunny, came to the Colony along with the handsomest boy I had ever laid eyes on. His name was Ben Barison.

Ben was tall with broad shoulders, dark curly hair, and a smile that could shame the stars from the sky. It was clear that every one of the girls in the Colony quickly fell under his spell. And it was equally clear that he could have had his pick of any one of us. For some reason, he chose me. I thought to myself, *why would he pick me? What's so special about me?* He clearly saw something, and boy was I glad that he did. He came straight toward me with that smile as though we had both swallowed magnets.

After that first day, Ben found his way over to the Colony all the time, and it wasn't long before we were in love—that first, sweet summertime love that no amount of wild horses could have stopped. We dated a long time—the entire summer! Of course, that's not long at all, but to a sixteen-year-old, that was ages. I knew he was older, about nineteen or twenty, but little else about him. But that didn't matter. I loved him, in that thick intense way, and he said that he was in love with me.

The Mohegan school held an end-of-the-summer party for everyone in the Colony. At that party, Ben asked if he could speak to me.

Me and Ben in 1931

"It's hot in here," he said. "Let's go outside and take a walk."

We walked along a path in the woods, then he stopped and took my hand in his.

"Let's get married," he said.

"Okay."

We started to walk toward his car.

"Where are we going to get married?" I asked.

"Everybody gets married in Niagara Falls, so we're going to get married in Niagara Falls, too."

"Okay."

Just as we approached Ben's car, my cousin Ben Halprin came along the path.

"Hello. Where are you two headed?"

"We're going to Niagara Falls to get married," I said.

"No, you're not," my cousin said. "I'm taking you home."

Strangely, I didn't put up a fuss, nor did Ben. My house was nearby, so my cousin calmly took my hand and walked me home, and that was that.

After that day, the summer wound down and families who didn't live on the lake went back to the city. Lenore and her boyfriend broke up. She ended up marrying someone else, and we lost touch. The Barisons went back to Brooklyn, and that was the end of my relationship with Ben. He wrote to me a few times, but we just sort of fizzled. I don't have any regrets, but I often wonder, if my cousin hadn't stepped out onto that path that day and intervened, would Ben and I have gone through with it? I have my doubts. If we ever got to Niagara Falls, which was very unlikely, without any suitcases, or money, or marriage license and blood tests at that time, who would have considered that a valid marriage? I think we would have eventually come to our senses. We might have driven a couple of miles, then turned around.

I was in school at the time, and Ben had already graduated and had a job. I don't know exactly what his profession was. It fascinates me that I never knew what he did, yet I was willing to drive off and marry him. What little I knew about Ben I learned from Bunny. She told me that he bought his sister (I didn't even know he had a sister) a spa—a whole spa in Westchester or New England someplace. So, obviously he had money. He sold his business which was some kind of factory that he founded. He evidently invented something important and manufactured it.

If Lenore hadn't tapped me on the shoulder that day in class, I never would have met her friends. And I never would have met Ben. Matty and Bunny married and remained very close friends with Ben all throughout his life. Years later, Bunny mentioned to me that Ben never married. I know in my bones that he loved me very much. The way that he told me that he loved me made me think I might have been "the one" for him. Was it because he and I didn't get married that day that he never married anyone else? Although we truly loved each other, I can't help but think that if Ben had seriously wanted to marry me, for real, he would have found a way. He would have continued to write to me and court me, and once I had graduated from high school, he would have married me.

I saw him two times after that summer. A few years after I was married, my husband and I were invited to go to a party for the people who lived in the Colony. Ben was there. I spoke to him briefly, but the small talk was awkward.

Many years later, my husband and I were invited to Matty and Bunny's son's bar mitzvah, and I saw Ben there. We said hello at the bar and made small talk again over a drink. It was clear that we still felt love toward each other, but we soon ran out of things to say.

Time is a quiet thief that pulls people away from one another. It reminds me of the song *Same Old Lang Syne* by Dan Fogelberg where he bumps into his old lover in the grocery store years later on Christmas Eve. There was so much they wanted to say to each other, but too much time had passed. After sharing a drink and reminiscing, their conversation dragged. So, they kissed and went their separate ways once more.

Ben died four years later. Bunny told me that he had suffered a massive heart attack and died instantly. He was just 50 years old. I think of him every now and then, and when I do, I'm suddenly transported back to that not-forgotten summer when we were young and happy and very much in love.

And I feel that old familiar pain.

Chapter Four

In 1933, when I was 18 years old, my former piano teacher, Ben Lieberman, asked me to write lyrics to a song he was composing. I had known him since I was a little girl, because he lived at the Colony, too, and I had taken piano lessons with him when I was about ten. Those lessons didn't last long. Shortly after I started, he called my mother and said, "You're wasting my time and your money. Forget it."

That didn't bother me. He was right. I was terrible. I am completely tone deaf, you see. Whenever we sang in a choir at school, the teacher asked me to stop trying to sing and just move my lips. Anyway, Mr. Lieberman and I remained friends. He had read some of my poetry and said to me one day, "I'd like you to write the lyrics, and I'll compose the music, and we'll write a song together." I named the song "I Don't Care," and these are the lyrics:

I Don't Care

Got the air
I don't care,
girls to love are really

not so rare.
There are more fish out in
the sea,
and the fishing, honey is free.

I declare
I don't care,
did you think I couldn't
take a dare
when you said you had
enough?
You didn't think I'd call
your bluff – but

So long – good bye – don't
want you to think I'll
pine and sigh.
So long – good bye – cause
nothing like this can
make me cry.

Big shock, the song never went anywhere. I blamed the music, and he blamed the lyrics. It was a fun project, nevertheless.

It was about that same time that my parents and I moved from the Colony to Queens where Papa had opened a fruit market. I had to finish my senior year at Richmond Hill High School. One day, some of my schoolmates invited me to a party in the city thrown by a boy they knew named Morty Dubovsky. We piled onto the subway and headed to the Upper West Side to a large brownstone on 87th Street and Central Park West. Little did I know, going to the party that night would change my life forever.

The party was held in the basement. I don't remember much about that night—how many people were there or if there was anything to eat or drink—except that it was so stifling in that basement I could barely breathe. A good-looking boy spotted me and walked over.

"Hello, I'm Morty."

"I'm Gladys."

"How are you enjoying the party?"

"It's too hot down here."

"Let's go upstairs and sit in my father's office. It will be much cooler up there."

I followed him upstairs into what appeared to be a doctor's office. While I looked around the room, Morty took a seat behind the desk. After a little small talk, he paused and smiled at me.

"Can I see you again?" he asked.

"I'm going to the country for the summer. We have a place on Mohegan Lake at the Colony."

"What a coincidence. I'm going to be working up there this summer as a counselor at a camp on Lake Mohegan right across from the Colony. So, can I call on you?"

All that summer, Morty rowed a rickety old boat across the lake just to see me. I was also seeing another boy at the time. My friend Norman had an artsy cousin named Jack "Yonk" Kling who introduced me to his actor friend, Reginald Wilson. Reggie was beautiful, smart, and kind. He used to cook dinner for me. I liked Reggie very much, but Morty was persistent. Reggie and I never broke up, because there was never any understanding that the two of us were boyfriend and girlfriend. By the end of the summer, it was simply as though my friendship with Reggie faded, and my friendship with Morty grew stronger.

My parents decided to move back up to Mohegan full time by

then, so I lived for a short while with my mother's sister, Rose Kane, and her husband, Joe. They had an apartment in the Bronx opposite the Yankee Stadium. The following year, my cousin and I and two of our friends rented a dinky apartment at 104th Street and Broadway. It was above an Automat, which was a cafeteria where all the food and drinks were served out of vending machines. I don't mean the free-standing vending machines you now see in offices today. These were wall-to-wall glass and chrome beauties that were often decorated in Art Deco embellishments. The Automat served freshly made food, and for a few coins, you could get a delicious meal and hot cup of coffee.[17]

I had enrolled at NYU and would come home from class and find clusters of people we didn't even know in the apartment. Apparently, they knew somebody who knew somebody who lived there. It was as though all of New York had a key to our place! Of course, I wouldn't dream of allowing that kind of open door policy in this day and age, but back then, it never bothered me that perfect strangers came in and out of our apartment at all hours of the day and night. In fact, one time, my cousin came to the apartment with a crowd of people in tow. They had been at a party where one of the games was a treasure hunt, so they came in looking for some object they needed. Living in that tiny apartment was fun. Swarming with people, but fun.

I never graduated from NYU. My relationship with Morty was getting serious, so I decided to drop out of the liberal arts program and instead enroll in a six-month course at the Merchants and Bankers' Business School. I thought being familiar with business was a good idea at the time.

On June 12, 1936, Morty and I were married. There was no fanfare or big proposal. We just decided to get married. That same year, he was accepted at the NYU School of Medicine. His father, Benjamin, had graduated from there, so it was assumed that Morty would naturally follow in his footsteps. His mother, Lena, had insisted that Morty study medicine and become a doctor. It wasn't as though Morty didn't want to practice medicine. In fact, he liked the idea. It was always something he was expected to do.

Me and Morty
(Or as I like to say, Bonnie and Clyde)

My father owned two acres of land in the Colony, and we asked if we could build a house on one of those acres. He agreed.

"If it only costs $100, will you supply the lumber?" Morty asked.

"Whatever it costs, I'll supply the lumber."

We got the lumber we needed, dug the foundation, and built the house ourselves. Morty was out of school during the summer, so that's when we worked on the house. It was meant to be a summer house, because it didn't have any insulation or heat.

My cousin, Pat Fried, was married to a budding architect named

George Nemeny who drew up the plans for the house. As it turned out, George became quite famous for his mid-century modern style of open, airy houses, and this was one of the first houses he ever designed.

Unfortunately, Morty and George weren't exactly on the same page. Morty would frame out the windows just where he wanted them during the day then head back to the city for the night. Then George would come home to the Colony at night, head over to our house, and move the windows completely around. Toward the end of the project, we walked through the house and realized there were no closets. Not one. I ask you, who doesn't put closets in a house? Apparently, they weren't aesthetically pleasing to George's design, but he begrudgingly put in a few. The whole building process was hit or miss to say the least, but we finally finished the house.

As it turned out, George was a rake. He cheated on Pat, his wife, any chance he got. He started seeing a very famous psychiatrist who seemed to make matters worse. One day, I suggested that Pat make an appointment to see this psychiatrist.

"All this doctor is getting is George's side of the story," I said. "You have to go and give him your side."

"I don't think it will do any good. Besides, he refuses to see me."

"You must insist."

She finally convinced the doctor to see her for a session. Pat was right. Seeing the doctor did no good at all.

"George is a creative genius," the doctor told Pat. "Everything is his life has to be subjugated to that creativity. If he needs to take a lover or two to do that, then you must accept that this is the only way."

Can you imagine that crap? This was a very famous doctor and that was the advice he gave her. Basically, she was told that she need-ed to put up and shut up. George continued to design many family homes and earned a number of architecture awards in the 1950s and 60s. His striking airy designs led to him being named one of the top 10 architects in the country. And he continued to sleep around, so Pat finally divorced him.

Morty and I started construction on our house in Mohegan in 1936, and we worked on it every summer until it was finally completed in the summer of 1938. Not long after our house was finished, my parent's house next door burned to the ground. Instead of rebuilding their house, they moved into our new house. My father always felt as though that house was his house, too. Morty and I moved into our house the summer of 1938 and lived with my parents. Before classes started back up in the fall, we moved in with his parents for the rest of the school year in the brownstone where we met on the Upper West Side. It was the most miserable time of my life.

Chapter Five

"Your mother insisted that I address her as Mother and your father as Father," I said as Morty and I got ready for bed.

"What's wrong with that?"

I sat in front of a mirrored dresser and brushed my hair. "It's so formal. And it's a little creepy."

"What do you want me to say?"

"Nothing."

Morty sat on the edge of the bed and fiddled with a button on his pajamas. "Mother insists that we all call them Mother and Father, although I'm sure Father would prefer to be called Dad. Whenever he writes to my brother and sister and me, he signs his letters 'Dad.' But none of us would dare cross Mother.

"Still, they're not my parents."

"Maybe it's because she loves you like a daughter."

Morty was overly optimistic about his mother's feelings toward me. Guaranteed Lena never thought of me as a daughter. Don't get me wrong. We didn't hate each other per se. We just never saw eye-to-eye. She may or may not have been pretty on the outside, but because she was so mean-spirited, I only saw her ugliness. A nastier

woman never drew breath. She was cruel and selfish and stingy when
she didn't have to be.

One afternoon, my mother and Aunt Rose came to the city to
see where I lived. The brownstone had five stories, and many of the
rooms were never used. There were never any kids over to play. It
was a huge, lonely house. As I was showing them through the place,
Lena came home, mounted the stairs, and found the three of us in
the living room. Her scowl was always the first thing to enter a room.

"Mother, I'd like to introduce you to my mother and my aunt,"
I said.

Mama and Aunt Rose stepped forward to shake her hand, but
Lena stood still.

"This is my house, and I issue the invitations," Lena said.

I was mortified. I saw Mama's eyes grow wide. They stepped
back, and Mama elbowed Aunt Rose. Without a word, the two of
them quickly left the house. None of my family came to visit me
there ever again. Whenever they came into the city to see me, I made
sure we met somewhere away from the house.

Just before my wedding, Aunt Rose gave me a beautiful white
satin robe for my trousseau. In the summer of 1939, Morty and I
went upstate to work for his aunt who had a bed and breakfast. I left
the robe behind in our room at Morty's house. I didn't want to take
it with me because it was too precious. When we came back home
at the end of the summer, Lena came toward me with something in
her hand. She had crumpled my robe into a ball and tossed it at me.

"Here, have this cleaned."

She had taken my cherished robe out of my closet and had worn
it. I never asked Morty to say anything to her, because he was working hard and was so busy with his studies. But I never wore my beautiful robe again. She had ruined it for me, so I threw it away.

I stayed out of the house most of the time either visiting friends, shopping, or going to the movies. I occasionally worked as a secretary for Morty's father, and that brought us closer. Before then, I thought he was standoffish, but the truth was, he was put off by his wife. She made it nearly impossible for him to have a close relationship with his children, and later on, she was instrumental in turning them all against him. She told them that he had been unfaithful to her. And he probably was, but who could blame him? It was clear that the two of them were miserable together. If Lena had been different, kinder and less severe, or if Ben had married someone else, things would have been better for him.

I liked him and thought that he was an interesting man. He was born in Talne, Ukraine and emigrated to the United States in 1905 when he was just thirteen. He had been a successful journalist and wrote for the Jewish Morning Journal when he met Lena. She insisted that he go back to school and become a doctor, because she was marrying a doctor and that was that. After he graduated from NYU medical school, he practiced medicine to please his wife, but continued to write. He wrote medical journals and published a piece each week in the Morning Journal about medical issues. He contributed to many other newspapers and magazines. He even wrote a book called Doktor bukh (Doctor's book). He published a book in English in 1948 under the name Dr. Benjamin Danniels called *Jesus, Jews and Gentiles: The True Story of Their Relationship as Recorded in the Bible.* Apparently, it stirred up controversy when it was published, but I have no idea why. He even studied the Quran.

He was an anarchist and told me the best stories.

"Did you know that Morty worked on a farm in Michigan when he was fourteen?" he asked.

"No, he never told me that."

He sat down behind his desk and leaned back in his chair. "I thought it would be good for him to experience life under anarchists."

I stopped filing papers and sat down.

"This farm was owned by two anarchists. They were trying to prove that it was possible to have a community without government. It was a complete commune—they grew their own food and had beautiful Percheron horses that won prizes. Morty said that everybody worked in the fields, and they grew melons. They ate melons morning, noon, and night! Anyway, the whole thing broke up because the two owners fought over which one of them was going to be the boss. So, that's the story of anarchism!"

I landed a job working in the Putnam Book Store. They were a publishing company, but they also ran a bookshop. Many of the publishers in those days like Scribner, Dutton, and Doubleday also had bookshops on or near Fifth Avenue. I worked in the Putnam Book Store library department making $10 a week. It was nice work, but unfortunately, I misunderstood when they hired me that it was only a temporary job for the Christmas season. I enjoyed it while it lasted, and I continued to write poetry:

1938

Ego

Your world in the shape of an I
Leaves horizons to you unbarred.
Your knowledge has limits on high,
By no fault is your mind left marred.

It must be weary for you indeed
To spend your life with such mortals as we.
So, my darling, I wish you Godspeed
To Valhalla where you can be free

Of such fetters imposed on you're here,
By those who respect not the wonder
Of having you with them, my seer.
Perhaps your peers will heed all your thunder!

December 1939

Love Poem

I

Shall I say
that my love is as swift
as a bird in its flight?
That my love is as strong
as the wind in its might?

That my love is as fierce
as the wild sun is bright?
That my love is as great
as wrong is from right?

That my love will last
as long as does Time?
My darling, these
are mere words that rime.

II

How can the glory of sun
in its heat
be told in that
which is rhythm and beat?

How can the beauty
of birds on the wing
be enclosed in a pen,
of their glamor to sing?

How can I dare
the strength of the wind,
explain it on paper,
lest its might be not dimmed?

III

My love is all this,
yea, much more, by far.
Yet ne'er can I tell you
for fear I would mar
its perfection.

You never will know
how much I love you.
For all I can say
is that I love you.

Morty never thought much about my poetry—not that that's a bad thing. I didn't ask for his encouragement nor did I need it, because I wasn't doing it for him. There were times when he was my inspiration, but it was never about him. It was something I did for me.

I wrote the following poem, *My Love*, in December 1939. To this day, most of my friends and family have requested that I recite this particular poem at their weddings. I happily obliged.

December 1939

My Love

I

If my love
Were a narrow cord,
Thrice would I surround the world and bring it you

If my love
Were turned to bread,
No more would man go hungry

If my love
Were turned to water,
Deserts would bloom forever green

II

But my love
Is a poor thing
I can give to you and only you.
So, take my love
And hold it tenderly,
For all that I would do for man
If I could change my love
Or if I could—would change it—
I will do for you.

III

I will give you a world.
The world of my love
Which encompasses all that I am and my dreams
can attain.

I will give you the bread
The stuff of my brain
As far and as wide as my mind can span—all my
innermost thoughts; they are yours

I will give you the water
My life's blood you may have
To refresh you. Ne'er again will you thirst

IV

But do not twist the cord,
Lest it should strangle us.
Nor turn the bread to cake,
Lest we fall sick of it.
Nor have the water changed to wine,
Lest we grow dizzy and forget
That humans must have water.

V

So, keep my love,
And give me in exchange
Your heart—wherein to store my gifts.

I showed my Uncle Joe my poetry. He was the vice president of the Bulova Watch Company at the time and knew the head of marketing at McCann-Erickson which is one of the world's leading advertising agencies at the time. Their head of marketing then showed my poem to the famous Irish poet, Oliver St. John Gogarty, whose only critique was that I ended a sentence with a preposition. He did say that my writing showed promise, so I continued to write.

When I wrote *Nought But This*, I was inspired by Elizabeth Barrett Browning and her poem *How Do I Love Thee?* from *Sonnets from the Portuguese.*

January 1940

Nought But This

What did Elizabeth give
Her love in gratitude and prayer?
She had a talent
So rich and so endowed
That in its name
She gave to him
A name made proud.

What can I give?
I who have not such talent.
Who have but this heart
Which beat for years
and knew not why it made my body live
Until that day
I saw your face
And my heart knew that it was ever yours.

Let that alone then
Give you pride
That you can call a soul to life
And give a heart its purpose.

I was unhappy at home and couldn't seem to find any solid foundation for myself intellectually or professionally. I had gone from my father's house where I was all but invisible to Morty's house where I was made to feel bothersome and disliked. Then I heard about Auden's class. I don't remember if it was through a friend or the newspaper, but as soon as I found out that he was to teach a class in New York, I thought to myself *My God, he's coming here. I just have to take that class!* It was February 1940, and this was Auden's first trip to the United States. He had just been appointed Poet Laureate. He was so famous that even the name for his century, the Age of Anxiety, was taken from the title of one of his poems.

The name of the course was *Poetry and Culture.* It was the only class Auden was teaching that semester. I didn't take the class for credit, because I wasn't even a student there. I'm not even sure if it was given for credit, because the course wasn't part of The New School curriculum. It was offered simply because he was coming to New York, and that was where he was going to be working.

On Wednesday afternoon, February 7, 1940, I boarded the subway to Midtown to West 12th Street and walked to The New School. I found the classroom—a huge amphitheater that held 250 students. There wasn't a desk or blackboard up front, but simply an empty stage as though we students were all seated in a theater about to see a play. I took a seat in the middle of the room and got out a spiral notepad and a pen. The air was charged as people shifted and murmured all around me. I didn't speak to anyone. I couldn't. I was too excited for small talk. To me, he was as sensational as the Beatles were to girls in another generation. The possibility of seeing him in the flesh thrilled me to the core. All I could think about was that Auden was in that building somewhere, and that at any moment, he would be in that room. Then suddenly, the room fell silent as Auden stepped out onto the stage.

W.H. Auden February 6, 1939, aged 32.

Carl Van Vechten photograph©Van Vechten Trust

Chapter Six

Wystan Hugh Auden was born in York, England, on February 21, 1907, and he grew up in Birmingham, England. He was the last of three sons born to George and Constance Auden and named after St. Wystan, a Mercian prince.[18] George was a medical officer for the city of Birmingham and a psychologist who not only studied the mind, but he also possessed extensive knowledge of mythology and folklore. Constance was a strict Anglican who was devoted to the Church of England. Both of his grandfathers were clergymen. Of his parents, Auden once wrote that, "Ma should have married a robust Italian who was very sexy. Pa should have married someone weaker than he and utterly devoted to him. But of course, if they had, I shouldn't be here."[19]

Because his father was a scientist and his mother was so religious, Auden was able to see the world, religion, and God in an almost metaphysical way. He rejected the notion of Hell as morally revolting and instead was determined to love thy neighbor as thyself. He even contemplated how the bacteria on his skin perceived God and made sense of the world around them. As shown in his poem, *A New Year Greeting*, Auden realized that in the eyes of the universe, we are as insignificant, and yet, as important as that bacteria.

> By what myths would your priests account
>> for the hurricanes that come
> twice every twenty-four hours,
>> each time I dress or undress,
> when, clinging to keratin rafts,
>> whole cities are swept away
> to perish in space, or the Flood
>> that scalds to death when I bathe? (lines 41-48)[20]

One afternoon in 1922 when Auden was fifteen, he and his fellow classmate at Gresham's School in Norfolk, Robert Medley, casually discussed the church. Robert was surprised to learn that Auden was religious. Embarrassed, he quickly changed the subject and asked Auden if he wrote poetry. Up until that point in his life, Auden had never thought much about writing poetry, but after that day, he realized that it was poetry and not religion where he found inspiration and fulfillment. His first published poems appeared in the school magazine in 1923.[21]

Years later while studying at Oxford, he became the central member of a group of writers called the "Oxford Group" or the "Auden Generation" which included Stephen Spender, C. Day Lewis, Louis MacNeice, and Christopher Isherwood who became Auden's good friend, literary mentor, and sometimes-sexual partner. The group supported the notion that the transition from capitalism to socialism was an inevitable part of the development of human society. Auden's first book of poetry titled *Poems* was privately printed by Stephen Spender.[22] He used the same title for a very different book published in 1930 by Farber and Farber.

On a warm summer evening in June 1933, Auden experienced

what he called a mystical experience. He had been sitting on a lawn after dinner with three colleagues, two women and one man. They were making small talk when all of a sudden Auden said that something profound happened to him. I should mention that none of them had been drinking any alcohol. Auden felt a powerful force invade him. He wasn't afraid and didn't resist it, but instead let the energy flow through him. He understood at once what was meant to love one's neighbor as oneself.[23] He didn't feel anything different toward his colleagues afterwards, but he realized that they, and all of humanity, were of infinite value, and that their existence must be exalted.

One night many years later at a café in Italy, Auden told a friend, Thekla Clark, that to him "Loving Thy Neighbor" was the most difficult commandment to obey.

"Wystan, just who is your neighbor?" Thekla asked him thinking, of course, all of mankind.

"Anyone who needs you," he said.

She mused later that being with Auden was like "playing tennis with someone who was a far better player—it improved your game."[24]

That same year the National Socialist German Workers' Party, or the Nazi Party for short, rose to power. About the Nazis, Auden wrote:

"The novelty and shock of the Nazis is that they make no pretense of believing in justice and liberty for all, and attack Christianity on the grounds that to 'Love one's neighbor as oneself' was a command fit only for effeminate weaklings."

"This utter denial of everything liberalism had ever stood for was arousing wild enthusiasm, not in some remote barbaric land outside the pale, but in one of the most highly educated countries in Europe.

Confronted by such a phenomenon, it was impossible any longer to believe that the values of liberal humanism were self-evident. Unless one was prepared to take a relativist view that all values are a matter of personal taste, one could hardly avoid asking the question: If, as I am convinced, the Nazis are wrong and we are right, what is it that validates our values and invalidates theirs?"[25]

It's frightening to see similar injustices happening today in Syria, Somalia, Myanmar, Nigeria, and Darfur just to name a few. We humans have the potential for such compassion—such greatness—but I'm afraid we are stupid, fickle beings doomed to relive our histories without learning the hard-fought lessons of the past.

In 1934, Auden traveled to Hungary for three weeks with a few friends. He wrote in a journal titled *In Search of Dracula* that he had half hoped that they all would find the Count and get interred. They crossed the Carpathian Mountain on their way to Transylvania, but along the way, one of his friends fell ill, so they had to give up their search for Dracula.

I imagine traveling with Auden was quite an adventure. For one thing, he was a very picky eater and often had plenty to say about the food. While driving over the Carpathian Mountains toward the Tatras Mountains, he wrote that he and his companions picked up a sausage "as big as a Michelin tyre (tire) and a local bottle of wine that tasted like sanitary fluid."[26]

For another thing, Auden was a terrible driver. While leaving Budapest on his way back to Vienna, he got hopelessly lost, and in the process, ran over a hen.[27] Much weeping ensued. Once while on his way to lunch in Shaftesbury with a former student, Michael Yates, his car bumped a "too leisurely cow" which landed in a ditch.[28]

In the summer of 1936, Auden had been invited to Iceland for a month to write a travel book. He wasn't enamored with Reykjavik because there was nothing to do but drink. Auden always enjoyed seeing new places, but he avoided the tourist traps. Instead, he wanted to spend his time getting to know the locals.

Unfortunately, he found the people there to be generally unambitious, unromantic, and unidealistic. Also, to his dismay, he found that there were a shocking number of Nazis living in Iceland. While on a bus to Lake Mývatn, he couldn't help but overhear the Nazis drone happily on and on about how Germanic Iceland was—how very Aryan all the people were, with their blonde hair and blues eyes. Auden laughed to himself when the bus passed by a couple of kids on the side of the road "who were as black as night."[29]

While visiting a farm in Egilsstaðir, Auden asked if he could ride the farmer's horse—the prize race horse of East Iceland. Before attempting to mount the creature in a courtyard filled with other horses and riders, he walked over and nervously clucked at the poor thing, which sent it hopping around, scattering the people and other horses in every direction. After he finally managed to mount the horse and steer it toward the road, it broke into a full gallop. Auden tried in vain to control it but gave up and held on for dear life. The farmer motioned Auden over after he returned to the stable.

"I'm very impressed with how well you handled the horse," the farmer said. "You must be a seasoned rider."

"Riding him was more exciting than any race car," Auden said.

The truth was, the first time Auden had ever been in the saddle had been the month before where he tried to mount a horse and flipped over its neck and crashed to the ground right in front of a bunch of picnickers. After finally maneuvering himself into the saddle, he sat upright, chin held high, and pictured himself as a regular he-man on his steed, that is until the horse took off running, and his high-pitched squeals for help nearly frightened a nearby English girl to death.[30]

Auden was a loving and generous man and a loyal friend. There are countless times when he performed acts of kindness, and in most cases, he wished to keep those acts anonymous. In 1935, Auden married the German Jewish actress Erika Mann so she could obtain British citizenship and avoid persecution from the Nazis. Erika first asked Christopher Isherwood if he would marry her, but he refused. Isherwood then cabled Auden and asked if he would marry her to help her out. The one-word cable came straight back: "DELIGHT-ED." She immediately travelled from Amsterdam to England and married him on June 15, 1935 at the Registry Office in Ledbury, Herefordshire.[31] Auden arranged the wedding reception at the pub near the school where he was teaching.[32] Despite the fact that they hardly knew each other at the time of their wedding, Mann and Auden became good friends. He dedicated his 1936 collection of poems *Look, Stanger!* to her. They never lived together but remained friends and technically married until her death in 1969 at the age of 63, leaving him $3000 in her will.[33]

Another time, Auden heard that a friend needed an operation that he couldn't afford. Auden invited the man to dinner. The operation never came up in conversation during dinner, but afterwards as the man was leaving, Auden said, "I want you to have this," and handed him a large notebook. It was his manuscript *The Age of Anxiety*. The University of Texas offered the man a pretty penny for the poem. He sold it and was able to have his operation.[34] That book-length poem won the Pulitzer Prize for Poetry in 1948 and inspired Leonard Bernstein to compose his symphony *The Age of Anxiety*.[35]

Another time, a Canadian burglar discovered some of Auden's poetry in the prison's library. He was so moved by the poems that he wrote to Auden who wrote him back. Not only did Auden respond to the man, but he gave him literature lessons.[36]

And yet another instance in the 1950s while attending St.

Mark's in-the-Bowery Episcopal Church on Second Avenue and 10th Street, Auden heard about a fellow parishioner, an old woman, who suffered night terrors. He went to her apartment with a blanket and slept outside her front door in the hall on the floor just so she would feel safe. [37]

In my favorite movie, *Casablanca*, we learn that Humphrey Bogart's character Rick fought for the Republicans in the Spanish Civil War. He left Spain and fled to his Moroccan café feeling defeated and cynical. In January 1937, Auden travelled to Spain, and instead of being welcomed as a liberal ready to do his part for the Republican cause working as an ambulance driver, he was instead put to work broadcasting propaganda. He was scorned and ignored because he wasn't a member of the Communist Party. Those seven weeks in Spain deeply affected him and his beliefs. He wrote,

> *"On arriving in Barcelona, I found as I walked through the city that all the churches were closed and there was not a priest to be seen. To my astonishment, this discovery left me profoundly shocked and disturbed."*

Barcelona's fifty-eight churches hadn't just been closed but burned or blown up and many of the priests systematically brutalized.

> *"The feeling was far too intense to be the result of a mere liberal dislike of intolerance, the notion that it is wrong to stop people from doing what they like, even if it is something silly like going to church. I could not escape acknowledging that, however, I had consciously ignored and rejected the Church for sixteen years, the existence of churches and what went on in them had all the time been very important to me. If that was the case, what then?"*[38]

What then, indeed.

On May 20, 1937, Auden's poem, *Spain*, was published in England. That very day, George Orwell, who incidentally had also been in Spain fighting on the front lines, was shot in the throat. Orwell later praised Spain as "one of the few decent things written about the Spanish War", however, he went on to criticize certain parts of the poem that described 'The conscious acceptance of guilt in the necessary murder.' Orwell believed that only someone who had never killed another man could have written words like these.'[39]

Auden later disavowed *Spain*, because he said he never personally felt those feelings or experienced the horrors he wrote about, so to him, the poem was deceitful. Then in 1940, Auden published *Spain 1937*, an altered version of the piece in his book of collected poems titled *Another Time*. It was controversial in part because of the marked differences between the two poems. It also shows a shift in Auden's philosophy about poetry and politics.

In 1937, Auden's book of poetry titled *Look, Stranger!* won the 1937 King's Gold Medal for Poetry. When presented to King George IV, he innocently asked him, "Did you like my book, sir?" Auden had no idea that one must never speak to a monarch unless spoken to. King George, a stammerer, was so shocked by the breach of protocol that he tried to say something in reply, but only managed to choke out a few guttural sounds. Auden, horrified and embarrassed, quickly bowed and walked away backwards, thankful the dreadful event was over.[40]

Many of Auden's poems written during the 1930s and afterwards were inspired by unconsummated love. Auden longed to find true love—an almost mystical love—but he never thought it would happen to him or that he would see it if he ever stumbled upon it. While traveling from Paris to Marseilles with Isherwood, Auden wrote *Twelve Songs Poem*. Here is an excerpt, number XII, about how he might stumble upon that love:

> When it comes, will it come without warning
>   Just as I'm picking my nose?
> Will it knock on the door in the morning,
>   Or tread in the bus on my toes?
> Will it come like a change in the weather?
>   Will its greeting be courteous or rough?
> Will it alter my life altogether?
>   O tell me the truth about love. (lines 49-56)[41]

As it turned out, when love came to Auden, it came without warning.

Chapter Seven

On the cold, snowy morning of January 26, 1939, Isherwood and Auden stood on the deck of a ship admiring the Statue of Liberty as they sailed into New York Harbor.[42] Within three months of coming to America, Auden would find the love of his life. On Thursday evening, April 6, 1939, he, Isherwood, and a few others had been asked by the League of American Writers to give a talk and poetry reading. In the audience that night were students from Brooklyn College's literary magazine the *Observer*. Three of the boys, Harold Norse, Walter James Miller, and Chester Kallman, sat in the front row. Chester, knowing very well that Auden and Isherwood were homosexuals, spent the evening flirting and winking at them. Afterwards, the boys went backstage and introduced themselves to Auden and Isherwood. Auden studied the handsome blonde Miller as he spoke with Isherwood about poetic drama and an essay that he had written on the subject.

"I couldn't help but overhear you say you wrote an essay," Auden interjected. "I'd like to read it if I may."

Auden had barely noticed Chester Kallman who had been interviewing him. Chester was the junior managing editor of the magazine. He was just eighteen and had wavy golden hair, grey-blue eyes and flawless skin the color of a Florentine angel.

"May we make an appointment to interview you properly?" Chester asked.

"Of course," Auden said. "You and your friend can come by our flat on Saturday."

That Saturday afternoon, Auden answered the door and saw that Chester had come alone.

"Please, come in. Have a seat in the living room. I'll be right with you."

Auden found Isherwood in the next room writing letters and gave him a look.

"It's the wrong blonde," Auden said, hoping Walter Miller would have shown up instead.

Auden returned to the living room for the interview. The son of a Brooklyn dentist, Chester Kallman was beautiful, funny, and vivacious. Although he might have been the wrong blonde at first, by the end of the afternoon, Chester had become the right one—the only one.[43] From that afternoon on, their relationship quickly blossomed.

In the spring of 1939, Auden left New York for Southborough, MA for a four-week guest teaching post at St. Mark's School. Auden wrote to Chester, and he in turn read Auden's letters out loud to his fellow classmates. Walter Miller said he remembered that Chester had written some poetry and asked Auden, "Do you think I have talent?" Auden wrote back, "You know as well as I do that there are hundreds of young poets sitting in attics writing poetry, and most of them are not going to make it. But established poets like me look upon this as a wave coming toward us!"[44] Auden was diplomatic and clearly didn't want to comment on Chester's poetry.

Chester was not shy about being gay. He was out and proud in a way that Auden had never encountered before. Auden never hid the fact that he was gay. He just never flaunted it, even though in England, it was illegal to be a homosexual. England has a long history of offenses against the LBGTQ community. As early as the 1st century during the Roman conquest of Britain, homosexuality was considered a crime. During the 12th century, King Henry VIII passed the *Buggery Act 1533* making all male-male sexual activity punishable by death. In the 19th century, Oscar Wilde was sentenced to two years hard labor for gross indecency.[45] In Auden's time and well beyond, people were persecuted and imprisoned for being gay. In 1954, Alan Turing, the English mathematician, logician, cryptanalyst, and Olympic-level runner was convicted of indecency. He was responsible for breaking the codes of the Nazi Enigma machine during World War II which, according to some historians, shortened the war in Europe by as many as two to four years. At a conservative estimate, each year approximately seven million lives were lost in that war. That would mean that Alan Turing saved an estimated 14 to 21 million people.[46]

Alan Turing saved millions of lives, and in the process, was instrumental in creating the modern-day computer, and yet, before the movie *The Imitation Game* came out in 2014, I had never heard of Alan Turing. Why weren't we taught about his great achievements in school? After his conviction of "gross indecency," he was given the choice of prison or house arrest where he would take female hormones in order to "cure" him of his homosexuality. In the final months of his treatment, the doctors ended the course of pills and inserted an implant of hormones into one of his thighs. The chemicals caused him to grow breasts and rendered him impotent. On June 7, 1954, Alan Turing killed himself by eating an apple laced with cyanide.[47]

Although he never flaunted his homosexuality, I can only imagine that being in the United States gave Auden a sense of freedom with regard to being gay. Of course, there are risks for gay men here, too. Even today, they have to put up with ignorant ridicule and the violence of hate crimes which at times results in injury or death. That said, simply being gay wasn't going to land him in jail in this country. In the two years since he had arrived, Auden went from a secretive head school master in England to the belle of the ball in the New York literary society. He and Chester partied on Fire Island with the rest of the sophisticated homosexual crowd. Fire Island, the New School, New York society, plenty of money from *Vogue,* and being head over heels in love with Chester. It must have seemed like Paradise.

His friend, Louis MacNeice, often joked that everything Auden touched turned to cigarettes. But the reverse can also be said—that he could turn cigarette ashes into poetry. Auden is known as one of the most prolific poets to ever put pen to paper, and he wrote so beautifully about everyday things such as rocks, bacteria, religion, psychoanalysis, death, and cooking. And he wrote about love. In the early days of his affair with Chester, Auden was inspired to write the most beautiful love poems. Here is just one of those poems about a man gazing at his sleeping lover. Auden juxtaposes love and death in the way he talks about his beloved as both "living" and "mortal." His focus on how fragile and finite our lives are, makes love seem all the more poignant and beautiful.

Lullaby

Lay your sleeping head, my love,
Human on my faithless arm;
Time and fevers burn away
Individual beauty from
Thoughtful children, and the grave

Proves the child ephemeral:
But in my arms till break of day
Let the living creature lie,
Mortal, guilty, but to me
The entirely beautiful.

Soul and body have no bounds:
To lovers as they lie upon
Her tolerant enchanted slope
In their ordinary swoon,
Grave the vision Venus sends
Of supernatural sympathy,
Universal love and hope;
While an abstract insight wakes
Among the glaciers and the rocks
The hermit's carnal ecstasy.

Certainty, fidelity
On the stroke of midnight pass
Like vibrations of a bell,
And fashionable madmen raise
Their pedantic boring cry:
Every farthing of the cost,
All the dreadful cards foretell,
Shall be paid, but from this night
Not a whisper, not a thought,
Not a kiss nor look be lost.

Beauty, midnight, vision dies:
Let the winds of dawn that blow
Softly round your dreaming head

> Such a day of welcome show
> Eye and knocking heart may bless.
> Find the mortal world enough;
> Noons of dryness see you fed
> By the involuntary powers,
> Nights of insult let you pass
> Watched by every human love.[48]

Life for Auden was perfect. But as they say, nothing lasts forever. One evening in 1939, he attended a German-language film in Manhattan. The United States had yet to declare war, so German films could still be freely shown in the theater. That film included an official German newsreel celebrating the Nazi victory over Poland. Suddenly, the peaceful audience of German immigrants started shouting at the screen "Kill the Poles!"[49] The audience's violent reaction shocked and frightened Auden. After that night, perhaps out of fear or a need for solace, Auden started attending church again. By the following year, he had made a habit of slipping out of the house early every Sunday morning and attending service at the nearby Episcopal church. It was his way of dealing with the horrors of Hitler's war.[50] He found that attending church again also gave him the chance to honor the two Jewish men in his life that he loved: Jesus of Nazareth and Chester Kallman of Brooklyn.

Regarding Europe from New York on the day that Germany invaded Poland, he wrote in his diary, "Such a beautiful evening and in an hour, they say, England will be at war."[51] It inspired him to write one of his most famous poems, *September 1, 1939*, which opens:

> I sit in one of the dives
> On Fifty-second Street
> Uncertain and afraid

As the clever hopes expire
Of a low dishonest decade:
Waves of anger and fear
Circulate over the bright
And darkened lands of the earth,
Obsessing our private lives;
The unmentionable odour of death
Offends the September night. (lines 1-11)[52]

On that same day in 1939, Auden wrote in his diary of how he "woke with a headache after a night of bad dreams in which C (meaning Chester) was unfaithful. Paper reports German attack on Poland ... 6.0pm." [53]

Little did he know it, but his bad dreams would soon come true. However, in 1940, W.H. Auden was on top of the world—he was deliriously happy, internationally lauded, professionally fulfilled, and very much in love.

Chapter Eight

You could have heard a pin drop on cotton as Auden stepped out onto the stage. No photo could have prepared me for his appearance. He was tall and gangly and wore brown slacks and a cream-colored cabled sweater. He was somewhat narrower in the shoulder than wider in the hip. His big ears jutted like sails through rusty-blonde hair that parted on the right and swooped over the top of his forehead. On his smooth face, a mole nestled onto his right cheek.

Auden introduced himself to the class, then bounded across the stage like a huge gander. I read that friends who dared to join him on his many walks had a hard time keeping up with him. His flat feet awkwardly propelled him in a crooked line, and as he traipsed forward, his arms and head jerked wildly about.[54]

There was absolutely nothing pretentious about the way he looked or carried himself. His friends often commented that Auden's manner of dress was "idiosyncratic, ill-fitting, and smelly." He often wore a black overcoat that draped over his body and came down to his knees—something most likely "rescued by him from one of his mother's jumble sales."[55] I later learned that while teaching at a British boy's school, the students thought their beloved teacher was "completely unconventional, striding about in a large black Flemish hat, waving an umbrella."[56]

In our class, there were no Q&As. Auden simply talked to us in a soft voice thick with accent, and we took notes. I could not have been more enchanted. No books were assigned. He just talked and we listened.

"A popular fallacy is that poetry must be a reflection of the age in which it is written," he said. "In that case, a poem must agree with one's beliefs. Let's say if a poem says that a fascist government is ideal, you must agree or the poem is valueless. So, you see, you cannot make an aesthetic judgment about art. A poet must believe that there is no right or left, just symmetrical and asymmetrical people. Poetry must be an agent for the future also. Doubt and faith will give a Double Focus which is essential to a poet, who must believe that any statement is a half-truth."

I had taken a course in shorthand, so I began writing down everything he said. I soon realized that I couldn't remember how to read it, so I stopped focusing on my notepad and simply observed him as he loped back and forth. Although he addressed a room filled with hundreds of students, it was as though he was speaking to each one of us individually.

"A poet must develop a sense of humor which will enable him never to believe a word he says and yet believe that a half truth will get him somewhere. Any statement is neither all true nor entirely untrue."

He paused and looked out at us.

"Writing involves bravery. One has to dig deeply and go to the dark spaces exposing the skeletons in the cupboards. If not, the reader will see you as a fake and call you out. One should be able to believe that if one wanted to, one could take his clothes off in the middle of Fifth Avenue. You wouldn't, but you should think yourself capable of it."

"Poetry must arise from the poet's experience. Yet emotions may be important in a man's poetry which have no importance in his life. A poet works in a medium—words. And words are a common property. Each poem is different to every reader, and yet it still must hold a common similarity to all."

He resumed his pacing and waving his arms.

"Let us compare Primitive Agricultural Tribes to that of the Nomadic Tribes. In the Agricultural Tribes, people settle down in one area. Culture in such a society would be a common belief and habit. In such a society, because people dwell in one area, there is a poetic tradition of expression, for example, there are certain ways of acceptable speech and actions within the tribe."

"The Nomadic Tribe differs, because those people aren't settled in one place. They travel, therefore they come into contact with many other people. The Nomadic Tribe has a belief in fate, because there is exposure to other's values."

"As civilization increases, there is an increase in diversity. The difference between people becomes more marked. And therefore, their art becomes more psychological."

After that first class, I took the subway home and spoke to no one. I expected to learn about poetry, but my mind swirled with Auden's words and concepts about civilization, culture, art, and life. It was as though every door suddenly unlocked, and the world broke open like an egg cracked and served sunny side up.

Chapter Nine

I n our subsequent classes, Auden spoke of the Greeks and Norse mythology, *The Golden Fleece*, *The Divine Comedy*, and *Cupid and Psyche*.

"Exaltation of women," he said, "did not come from Germanic races. Women gained equality but not idealization. Neither did it come from the church. Worship of Mary came from that rather than vice versa. The exaltation of women came from feudal tradition. To pray is to pay attention or, shall we say, to 'listen' to someone or something other than oneself.

I was inspired to write this poem:

March 1940

Prayer

Give me no Heaven
Where my soul may rest.
I wish no release
From evil. Don't put me to the test!

Let me lie quiet
When my battle is done.
Don't make me strive eternally
For more battles to be won.

I will not spend eternity
Clad in a harp and wing.
Just let me rest in peace
And hear the other angels sing!

William Blake was a mystic poet, painter, printmaker, and visionary of the Romantic period. Auden discussed Blake's *The Marriage of Heaven and Hell*. Blake saw concepts such as heaven and hell, good and evil, as potentially limiting systems of understanding. Sin exists only in the repression of human desire. Blake's views were a direct contradiction to Christian ideology in that he believed that transgressions were necessary for growth, and that sin was a necessary constituent of the divine within Man.

Blake was trained in his youth as a draughtsman and an engraver although he would have preferred a career as a painter.[57] He produced a print that Auden spoke of titled *Newton*. Blake's Isaac Newton is pictured naked and crouched on a rock submerged under the sea. He is bent over what looks like a map with a compass in his hand. Auden pointed out that Blake's painting is meant to criticize Newton's world view as he is so focused on his scroll and compass that he completely misses the beauty of the nature all around him. Blake went so far to declare that "Art is the tree of life. Science is the tree of death."[58]

Interestingly, Blake's 1794 painting, *The Ancient of Days,* was sold to A.E. Newton's daughter, Caroline Newton, who gave it to W.H. Auden in 1941. Upon his death in 1973, the painting was then bequeathed to Chester Kallman.[59]

Auden also spoke to us of the English poet, John Milton, who wrote at a time of religious flux and political upheaval. He was best known for his epic poem *Paradise Lost* in which the subject is Man's disobedience and the ensuing loss of Paradise on earth, but its theme in the simplest term is love. In Book IV, Milton shows the true beauty of Adam and Eve's love for each other and how they are the perfect compliments to one another:

> Hee for God only, shee for God in him:
> His fair large Front and Eye sublime declar'd
> Absolute rule; and Hyacinthin Locks
> Round from his parted forelock manly hung
> Clustring, but not beneath his shoulders broad:
> Shee as a vail down to the slender waste
> Her unadorned golden tresses wore
> Disheveld, but in wanton ringlets wav'd
> As the Vine curles her tendrils, which impli'd
> Subjection, but requir'd with gentle sway,
> And by her yielded, by him best receivd,
> Yielded with coy submission, modest pride,
> And sweet reluctant amorous delay. (lines 299-311)[60]

To find that perfect love in another is a miracle. Those of us who are blessed to find love know its immeasurable value. Unfortunately, not all of us are as fortunate. This poem that I wrote wasn't inspired by anyone in particular. It just came to me:

March 1940

Cry of an Intellectual Spinster

The books upon my shelves are cold.
They stand as if left by a mold.
A colored pattern, stiff with import.
Each with literary value frought.
Each placed in line.
There they are: collection saturnine.
No warmth, no laughter to impart.
They feed my mind—what of my heart?
What have these sweethearts of my brain
to weight the scales a lover can't disdain?
What husbands these who so distort
a mating?   And I bear forth...a thought!

Toward the end of the semester, Auden said at the end of one of the classes, "If anyone has a poem that they would like me to critique, please pass it forward." So, I passed my poem, *My Love,* up to the front of the class.

The following class, Auden started by asking, "Is there a Gladys Lee here?" I raised my hand.

"Can you please meet me tomorrow at Stewart's Cafeteria at one o'clock? I'd like to discuss your poem."

I find it impossible to believe that I was the only student that Auden chose to meet with. And yet, for the life of me I cannot remember him commenting on anyone else's poems or asking any other student in the class to personally meet with him. That doesn't mean that he didn't. I simply don't recall him ever addressing anyone else in the class. I guess that's what I find so unimaginable—that I would be the only one out of 250 students that that great man sin-gled out and chose to speak with. The mind reels.

When I woke up the following morning, I had no idea that my conversation with Auden that afternoon would affect me in such a monumental way—that it would be a watershed moment in my life that would permanently change the way I felt about myself.

Chapter Ten

Two famous gay outposts in Greenwich Village, The Life Cafeteria and the lower-priced Stewart's Cafeteria, faced each other across Sheridan Square. Stewart's Cafeteria was located at 89 Christopher Street on the corner of Christopher and Seventh Avenue South. Today, it's a General Nutrition Center, but back then it was a very popular restaurant. It seemed as though everyone in the gay community ate there. You could get a whole meal and a view for as little as .75 cents.

Stewart's Cafeteria in May 1933.
Photo by Percy Loomis Sperr ©Milstein Division
The New York Public Library

I entered Stewart's Cafeteria and wove through a flock of handsome gay men in stylish clothes, light make up, and exquisitely coiffed hair. Straight tourists crowded outside on the sidewalk and pressed their faces against the large plate-glass windows in order to catch a glimpse of the patrons as though those of us inside the restaurant were trapped in a fish bowl.

I found Auden sitting at a table drinking tea. A cigarette was pinched between his fingers, thick and yellow like old piano keys. His nails had been bitten down to the quick and stained with tobacco and ink. He was seldom without a cigarette and often joked with his friends that his need to suck something was probably a result of not being properly weaned.[61] In addition to his chain smoking, I had heard that he had a habit of drinking a dozen cups of tea a day. He rose when he saw me and motioned for me to sit down. His eyes were soft and beautiful, and in their amber depths was a profound sadness.

He pulled my poem from a tired leather satchel and smiled at me. He had such a kind, gentle face. Years later, that same creamy face would become deeply lined and cluttered with folds. Some thought it was because of his smoking habit or his love of the Italian sunshine. He himself described his face as tragic— "Like a wedding cake left out in the rain." In truth, he had a rare hereditary skin disease known as Touraine-Solente-Golé Syndrome, or pachydermoperiostosis, or the elephant skin disease.[62] That's not to be confused with the Proteus Syndrome, which was the skin condition that Joseph Merrick known as "The Elephant Man" suffered from.[63]

He brushed the cigarette ash from his trousers, webbed with wrinkles. He crossed his legs and picked up his teacup.

"I'd like to talk to you about your poem, *My Love*," he said. "I'd like to ask you about this stanza here."

He pointed to the second stanza that ends:

If I could change my love
Or if I could—would change it—
I will do for you.

"What did you mean by that?" he asked.

"Well, I wasn't sure that I was ready to commit my love, my whole heart and soul, to one person, as in a long-term relationship or marriage. And also, I did it for the rhythm."

"Hmmm."

He never came out and said that he liked my poem, but that didn't matter to me. He didn't have to say it. The fact that he had chosen it, and that I was sitting there with him discussing it was proof enough for me that he liked it.

He had brought the January issue of *The Atlantic Monthly* with him. He thumbed through the magazine and found a poem that he had written called *Letter to Elizabeth Mayer* that had been published that month.

He met Elizabeth Mayer in September 1939. His friend, Benjamin Britten and his lover, the British tenor Peter Pears, were on a ship coming to America from England where they met the German refugee, Elizabeth Mayer. She was fleeing Nazi Germany with her children and going to Long Island to meet up with her husband the Jewish psychiatrist, Dr. William Mayer. As it turned out, Elizabeth loved the company of artists. She had opened her home in Munich to musicians and painters. In fact, she had wanted to study music herself, but that didn't suit her blue-blooded father.

He had arranged for her to marry a well-bred man, but she refused, wanting to marry the Jewish Dr. Mayer. So, she surrounded herself with artists and lived vicariously through them.

She invited Britten and Pears out to their home in Amityville, NY. On September 4th, Britten brought Auden out with them, and from that day forward, Auden and Elizabeth became fast friends. She was much older than Auden in both years and attitude. She reminded him of his dear mother back home and referred to her as his "Dearest and Best of Fairy Godmothers."[64]

After we talked about Elizabeth and discussed the poem he had written about her, he ripped it out of the magazine and handed it to me. I still have those pages in the folder where I keep my poems. Years later, my son, Dan, asked me why I didn't ask Auden to sign it. It never occurred to me at the time to ask him, but you can bet I'm kicking myself now!

After discussing his poem, our conversation went from anywhere to everywhere. At one point, we talked about James Joyce.

"I have to tell you, I don't approve of how Joyce writes," I said. "If he has something to say to me, he has to say it so I can understand it and not in private symbols."

Auden sipped his tea. "Well, I believe that James Joyce is way ahead of his time."

"Nevertheless," I said, "I don't think he has any right to write the way he does. There's no reason to."

"There will come a day when you will understand him and accept him more than you do right now. I don't believe most people are ready for him yet."

I'm 102 years old, and I still don't get Joyce. Apparently, he's still way ahead of his time. I once took a course on Ulysses simply because of my conversation with Auden. Still, nothing.

There I was questioning the greatest poet on earth at the time. I was actually arguing with him! All the while I was thinking what am I doing arguing with this great man, but I couldn't help myself. The astonishing thing was, Auden listened to me, and he spoke to me as if I were his equal. I mean, I said outrageous things about James Joyce, but he listened to me and answered me. He genuinely respected my opinion.

"Gladys, you're a very good poet. In fact, you could be a great poet—greater than me even. You need to stop everything you're doing and devote your life entirely to poetry."

I was stunned. I later learned that Chester Kallman had asked Auden in letters what he thought about his poetry. Auden wasn't prepared to commit to his lover's poetry, and yet, there I was, a perfect stranger, a nobody to him, and he was telling me that I could be great—even greater perhaps than him. It was more than I could take in.

Auden knew the value of discipline. He was successful in dedicating himself so fully to his poetry, because he had an incredible work ethic. By four o'clock, he had finished his work for the day, which gave him time to enjoy his tea before the evening's drinking commenced. He was a heavy drinker and had no problem announcing to the world that he was a drunk.

According to him, being a drunk and being an alcoholic were two different things. "When alcoholics drink, their behavior changes. Drunks' behavior stays the same." Nevertheless, no matter how much he drank the night before, he was up and at work again the following morning at 6:00. His long-time secretary, Charles H. Miller, once said that Auden was the least lazy man he had ever met.[65]

"Gladys, you can be anything you want to be in this world," Auden said. "You can do anything you want. There's a price on everything. Some people have to pay a lot, and other people get things for bargain prices. But you can do anything you set your mind to."

In the end, I decided not to dedicate my life to poetry, but I took his words to heart. From that day forward, whenever I set my mind to doing something, I knew I could get it done. Auden gave me the confidence to know that I could achieve anything I wanted to do in this life. It was the best advice anyone has ever given me, and his words live in my heart still.

I didn't believe him when he, this great, famous poet—the Poet Laureate—was telling me that I could be a great poet like him. I still don't have any doubts about my decision, nor do I have any regrets about the life I have chosen. I was right. And he was wrong.

But then again, you never know.

The thing that I got out of that whole experience was that his encouragement gave me self-confidence. His encouragement and advice were genuine, and I knew without a doubt that he believed in me. I sat there across from that great man, and he spoke to me like I was his equal, and it was clear that I mattered. I mattered to him. And I had never felt that I had mattered to anyone in my life up until that point. I mattered to him, and that's what mattered most to me.

Chapter Eleven

Our last class was held on April 10th. Auden discussed Wagner's *The Ring Cycle* and *Tristan und Isolde*.

"Wagner was a great decadent," Auden said, traipsing across the stage, "on a level with Proust and Joyce. His characters do not accept logical obligations of the oppressed and bourgeois classes."

Auden paused. "If you ask me, Wagner is a bit of a masturbatory artist." The class chuckled, and he resumed pacing. "That said, he produced magical representations of the world full of great truths and beauty. His characters are all like you and me—his stories are our love potion in real life, Saturday Evening Post, and the like."

The Ring Cycle is a long and passionate opera comprised of four different operas: *Das Rheingold, Die Walküre, Siegfried,* and *Götter-dämmerung*. Its intensity can be overwhelming. The story is about a magic ring that is stolen from the dwarf, Alberich, by Wotan, King of the Gods. Wotan has it stolen from him by two giants. Most of the story is about Wotan trying to steal the ring back. Of course, there are many characters, settings, and subplots, which require a serious orchestra, incredible sets, wonderful music, and a crazy storyline... all for a little piece of jewelry. It took Wagner about twenty-six years to complete the whole thing.[66]

I find it very interesting that Auden picked *Paradise Lost, Cupid and Psyche*, and *Tristan and Isolde* and their themes to discuss. It's as though he was comparing, and perhaps justifying, his relationship with Chester with these mystical stories. Maybe he saw his and Chester's love as something divine, other-worldly.

Paradise Lost is an epic poem that tells the story of rebellion and treachery, of innocence pitted against corruption, of the struggle between good and evil. At the heart of the poem are Adam and Eve who find themselves tempted. They give in to their frail human imperfections, and their unyielding love and trust lead to their fall from grace.

In the story of *Cupid and Psyche*, Cupid (in this case Auden) falls irrevocably in love with Psyche's (Chester) loveliness and charms. Despite Psyche's betrayal, Cupid continues to love and support her. At one point, Psyche opens a forbidden box and is overcome with a sleep so strong, it's as though she is dead—the same sleep of the dead we see in Sleeping Beauty and Romeo and Juliet. Cupid comes to rescue Psyche and lifts her sleeping body to the heavens.[67] It reminds me of Auden's poem *Lullaby* where the writer gazes upon his lover as he sleeps.

Tristan and Isolde is the story of two doomed lovers. Tristan was born to an important family and grew to be skilled in the arts and music. His uncle, King Mark, was old and unmarried. Fearing there would be no heir, Tristan suggested that the king marry the beautiful Irish Isolde.

Fearing Isolde would be put off by the king's old age, her mother prepared a love potion for the two of them to drink. Unfortunately, it was Tristan and Isolde who drank the potion disguised as wine. They fell madly in love. Isolde's maid told the pair that they had mistakenly drunk a love potion to assure Isolde's love for the king.

Tristan, faithful to the king, convinced Isolde to go through with the marriage anyway. Although she married the king, Tristan and Isolde were still under the potion's love spell and began an affair behind the king's back. When their affair was discovered, Tristan left the kingdom and married another woman named Isolde of the White Hands, but because of his undying love for the Irish Isolde, their marriage was never consummated.

After being mortally wounded in a battle, Tristan asked that his true love come and heal him. He told the messenger to hoist a white flag up the ship's mast so he could tell that she was on the ship. If she had refused, a black flag was to be raised.

Isolde of the White Hands saw the white flag on the ship. Jealous of her husband's love for the Irish Isolde, she told him that a black flag had been raised. Believing that his love no longer loved him, Tristan gave up the will to live and instantly died. Isolde arrived moments later to find her love dead. She held him in her arms and life drained from her body. Like Romeo and Juliet, Isolde died in Tristan's arms. And like Romeo and Juliet, their love was doomed here on earth.[68]

Perhaps Auden felt, as in these stories of ill-fated lovers, that the true love he found in Chester was not going to be realized here on earth, but that they were meant to be together forever in the afterlife.

At the end of the class, Auden stood front and center on the stage and looked out at us, taking in the faces of his students.

"Everyone's experience is modified by the culture in which he lives," he said. "Experience is no good until you've digested it. Absorb what comes into your mind, and let it sift itself. One takes into one's mind only what one wants to take in. The danger is that realization of this may make one forget to observe. Never forget to observe."

He smiled. "I wish you all the very best. Thank you for your time." He nodded, turned, and walked off the stage. We weren't given a final exam or assigned any grade. Auden simply wished us well, and we filed out of the auditorium.

I've heard it said that our lives are like individual fibers in a big cosmic tapestry. Our lives' threads weave together, separate, and run parallel or completely opposite one another, and many times, come back around to intertwine again. We meet, spend time together, and sometimes drift apart. We are all being influenced by those we encounter, and in turn, we influence others—many times without even knowing it.

I want to make it clear that I did not have a relationship with Auden. In fact, I never spoke to him again after that day in Stewart's Cafeteria or saw him again after the class ended. And yet, I have always held a soft spot in my heart for him. I loved him. After the class, I continued to read his poetry, and I kept track of what was happening in his life. And now, so many years later, I realize how many times my life's experiences and his ran parallel, separated, then crisscrossed again. Is it simply coincidence? Maybe. One thing is certain: his crossing my path changed me forever.

Chapter Twelve

In 1940, Auden moved into a jerry-rigged townhouse at 7 Middagh Street in Brooklyn Heights with George Davis, then the literary editor at *Harper's Bazaar*, writer Carson McCullers, composer Benjamin Britten, and Peter Pears. It was nicknamed the February House because so many of the tenants had birthdays in February.

George Davis complained that there was never any heat, the banisters wobbled, and the wind wheezed through the gaps in the windows. Nevertheless, he slowly made repairs and furnished the place in his own eclectic style: framed Valentines; a sofa with buffalo-horn armrests; and a grand piano donated by the editor-in-chief of *Harper's Bazaar*, Diana Vreeland.

Auden believed the best way to keep one's health and sanity was through routine—eating meals on time and getting to bed early. Unfortunately, the house was in a constant state of disarray. Nothing worked, there was never any hot water, and dirty dishes were forever heaped in the kitchen sink. He tried to organize the place, but to no avail. Writer James Stern dropped by one time to find "George naked at the piano with a cigarette in his mouth, Carson on the floor with half a gallon of sherry, and Wystan bursting in like a headmaster announcing: 'Now then, dinner!'"[69]

America's favorite stripper and Davis's close friend, Gypsy Rose Lee, rented a room on the third floor and offered to clean the house if Davis would teach her to write. Rumors spread of the odd collection of characters at the house and their crazy antics: Pears and Davis performing a ballet to 'Petrushka' up the curtains and the hot water pipes; parties which included Brooklyn pimps and sideshow performers along with the composers, playwrights, and painters; overnight visitors raiding the icebox at midnight and eating the cat food by mistake.[70] Auden called the house 'our menagerie', and at one point the residents included a trained chimpanzee with his keeper and an inmate who specialized in the parlor trick of inserting a cigarette in his anus and puffing out smoke.[71]

Despite the house's constant state of chaos, Auden had never been happier. Chester was by no means in Auden's league, however, he was charming, handsome, and energetic. He loved music, especially the opera, could cook, and loved sharing gossip. To outsiders, they didn't seem like a good match. But when it comes to love, the heart knows no logic. They traveled together, hosted dinner parties where Auden was forever walking around in bedroom slippers and attended the opera once a week where he'd slip his shoes off and stretch his stockinged feet during the performance, much to the chagrin of his fellow opera goers.[72] Auden was accepted and welcomed into Chester's family. He recognized in Chester not only a friend and lover, but a spiritual companion. Auden had finally found the romantic love he had been searching for his whole life. He loved Chester completely and believed himself to be loved in return.

The French, who understand love so very well, both its bright and bitter sides, give romantic love four years at best. Auden's romance with Chester started with such passion and promise in the spring of 1939 and ended in a nightmare two years later.

He was a tall, handsome sailor from England named Michael John Eustace Barker, although his friends called him Jack Barker. He had been considered the black sheep of a blue-blooded family, born on the ancestral estate outside Derby on July, 9, 1915 as the son of Lieutenant-General Michael Barker. He was educated at Cheltenham and then at Oxford, but never finished college. After dropping out, he became a sailor and an off-and-on journalist.[73]

In the autumn of 1940, Jack sailed from England on a British merchant ship into New York harbor. A mutual friend, presumably Stephen Spender, had given him Auden's telephone number and address to look up once he arrived. Jack called Auden who agreed to meet him for dinner.[74] Afterwards, the friendly and hospitable Auden invited Jack to stay at the February House in Brooklyn Heights. When Chester dropped by for a visit, he took one look at the sailor, with his olive skin, almond eyes, and perfect body, and fell head over heels in love. With Chester, each time he fell in love it was always for the first time. Auden never told Jack that he and Chester were lovers, because he didn't think it was necessary. Auden was so blindly in love that he never imagined for a moment that Chester would stray.[75] But stray he did.

Jack needed to go to *The New Republic* to type up one of his articles, and Chester asked if he could come along. That afternoon, after both Jack and Chester's mutual flirtations and Chester's blatant advances, the two of them escaped to a friend's house to be alone and have sex.

Jack sailed back to England, however, those months away from New York made him realize that he was in love with Chester. He returned to New York and resumed their affair. Just before he had to set sail again for Glasgow, he and Chester met in a bar to say goodbye.

"Before you go, I need to make something clear," Chester said. "I'm in a serious relationship with Wystan. He must never find out about our affair."

Jack was upset at the thought of two-timing Auden and told Chester that either they come clean and tell Auden of their love, or that he must back out and never see Chester again. Chester was so terrified of losing Auden that he begged Jack not to tell him. Jack sailed back to England without saying a word to Auden.[76]

It's not clear how Auden found out about the affair, but most likely guilt got the better of Chester and he confessed. Understandably, Auden did not take the news well. After their fight, Chester went to his bedroom, threw himself onto his bed, and went to sleep. Later that night, Auden, still enraged, crept into Chester's bedroom, wrapped his thick fingers around Chester's throat, and squeezed hard. Chester managed to fight him off and fled the room.

Auden was terrified by the realization that he was actually capable of murder. He took a step back and reconsidered his relationship with Chester. He knew that, despite the infidelity, he would always love him. At the same time, Chester truly loved Auden and didn't want to lose their friendship. Auden wanted a traditional, comfortable marriage in every sense of the word, which Chester was simply incapable of giving him. In the end, they both agreed not to end their friendship, but to live as roommates in a loving yet platonic relationship.[77]

Jack returned to New York after Auden and Chester's breakup, and Auden asked Jack to meet with him. Jack remembers their meeting as "positively Kiplingesque" and quite English. Auden was gentle and forgiving.

"Tell me that Chester was innocent," Auden said.

Jack took that to mean that Auden wanted to be reassured that he had been Chester's one and only fling. Jack knew that Chester was far more sexually experienced than the two of them combined, but he lied to Auden.

"As far as I know, Chester had remained innocent."[78]

The truth was, Chester was a bit of a slut who had a habit of picking men up from the street, in the harbors, and in the Brooklyn shipyards. He had been cheating on Auden long before Jack came on the scene. He was "a butterfly, incapable of sexual fidelity."[79]

I read about Chester's cheating ways years later, and it made me think of the stanza in my poem, *My Love*, that Auden had picked out to discuss with me:

> If I could change my love
> Or if I could—would change it—
> I will do for you.

I find it interesting that this is the part of my poem that intrigued Auden. It made me wonder, *why that stanza?* Did Auden subconsciously suspect that Chester was cheating on him? At the time when he read my poem, Chester hadn't yet confessed to cheating. Yet, on September 1, 1939, he wrote in his diary that he "woke with a headache after a night of bad dreams in which C (meaning Chester) was unfaithful. There had to have been something niggling in the back of his mind which caused him to doubt Chester's fidelity. Would Auden have liked to have changed Chester in some way? Or to change himself? When Chester finally confessed that he had been cheating, Auden was blindsided. Never underestimate the power of denial.

Despite their breakup, Auden remained loyal to Chester, even defending his cruel behavior. He would give Chester money only to have him turn around and waste it on his boyfriends. On one occasion, Stephen Spender met Auden and Chester for lunch at an outdoor café when Chester suddenly stood up, crossed the street, and began to hit on another young man. Spender watched as Auden seemingly ignored what Chester was doing across the street and continue his conversation with tears streaming down his cheeks.[80]

Chester was lazy. He refused to hold down a job and took full advantage of Auden's generosity. He certainly wasn't in the same artistic or academic league as Auden. You would think he would have dumped Chester and moved on, but Auden decided to stay when he clearly didn't have to. Obviously, there was something in their relationship that Auden appreciated, and that's why he chose to maintain it. Even though Chester at times could appear uncaring, even cruel, he was equally devoted to Auden.

Their new arrangement may have been something that Auden had accepted, but the rest of his friends and housemates resented. They disliked Chester for the way he treated Auden. They felt that he was insufficiently grateful for that great poet's love, kindness, and generosity. Chester was determined to make people see that he was Auden's equal. Unfortunately, no one shared Chester's lofty view of himself, and they made it painfully clear just where he stood in their eyes.[81]

Auden had always believed that being one's friend meant you had to accept both the good and the bad. If he was able to come to terms with Chester's promiscuity and the end of their sexual relationship, then his friends needed to accept that as well. The last straw for Auden's housemates came when both Chester and Jack Barker, who had been staying at the Middagh Street house, were diagnosed with syphilis. The outraged household drove Chester and Barker out of the house as though they had "the mediaeval plague."[82]

The summer of 1941 was a cruel one for Auden. In late August while visiting a friend in Rhode Island with Chester, Auden received a telegram which was read over the telephone to their friend, Caroline Newton. Auden's mother, Constance Rosalie Bicknell Auden had died in her sleep at home in Birmingham, England. Caroline told Chester, who then went to Auden's bedroom to break the news. They had planned to go to a party that night, which Auden had dreaded.

"We don't have to go tonight," Chester said.

"Goody, goody."

"You see, there's been a telephone call from England. Your mother has died."

Auden sat quietly for a long time. Finally, he looked at Chester. "How like her that her last act on earth should be to get me out of a social engagement that I didn't want."[83]

Understandably, Auden was shocked and deeply saddened by his mother's death, but that feeling of loss and despair was only compounded by the fact that just one month prior, his world had come crashing down after learning of Chester's infidelity. Auden would later write, "When one's mother dies, one is, for the first time, really alone in the world and that is hard."[84] Even though Chester proved to be a terrible romantic life partner, he remained a faithful friend, especially in times of need. He was compassionate and attentive to Auden during that sad time. In fact, Auden later commented that he didn't think he could have gotten through his mother's death without Chester by his side to support him.[85]

It's been said that 1941 has been described as the year that everything changed nearly down to the roots of life. After Pearl Harbor, December 7th came to symbolize, in Churchill's words, not only "the end of the beginning of the Second World War and the beginning of the end, but the end of one era in America and the beginning of another."[86]

By late December 1941, Auden seemed to have come to terms with the end of his old life with Chester and the beginning of their new arrangement. He wrote the following letter, which was discovered in the laboratory of Dr. Kallman's office sometime in 1946. It tells the real story of Auden and Chester's relationship:

Christmas Day. 1941

Dearest Chester

Because it is in you, a Jew, that I, a Gentile inheriting an O-so-genteel anti-Semitism, have found my happiness:
   As this morning I think of Bethlehem, I think of you.

Because it is you, from Brooklyn, who have taught me, from Oxford, how the most liberal young man can assume that his money and his education ought to be able to buy love;
   As this morning I think of the inn stable, I think of you.

Because, suffering on your account the torments of sexual jealousy, I have had a glimpse of the infinite vileness of masculine conceit;
   As this morning I think of Joseph I think of you.

Because mothers have much to do with your queerness and mine, because we have both lost ours, and because Mary is a camp name;
   As this morning I think of Mary I think of you.

Because the necessarily serious relation of a child to its parents is the symbol, pattern, and warning of any serous love that may later depend upon its choice, because you are to me emotionally a mother, physically a father, and intellectually a son;
   As this morning I think of the Holy Family, I think of you.

Because, on account of you, I have been, in intention, and almost in act, a murderer;

As this morning I think of Herod, I think of you.

Because even *les matelots** and *les morceaux de commerces*** instinctively pay you homage;
As this morning I think of the magi, I think of you.

Because I believe in your creative gift, and because I rely absolutely upon your critical judgement;
As this morning I think of the Godhead, I think of you.

Because in the eyes of our bohemian friends our relationship is absurd;
As this morning I think of the Paradox of the Incarnation I think of you.

Because our love, beginning Hans Anderson, became Grimm, and there are probably even grimmer tests to come, nevertheless I believe that if only we have faith in God and in each other, we shall be permitted to realize all that love is intended to be;
As this morning I think of the Good Friday and Easter Sunday already implicit in Christmas day, I think of you.[87]

*This refers to the sailors that Chester often picked up in bars along the harbor
**Pieces of trade was a camp name for pickups (usually heterosexual) in tough bars

After it became clear that Chester would never be faithful, Auden's dream of sharing a traditional married love with him was shattered. Yet in some way, he welcomed this new loneliness, and from then on, made his suffering and sacrifice the center of his artistic life.

Chapter Thirteen

In the fall of 1941, Morty started an eleven-month residency in Brooklyn and roomed with a man named Julius Kaufman whom we all called Julie. After their internship, both Morty and Julie enlisted in the Army to serve our country as doctors. We traveled to York, PA for their four-week basic training, and the three of us got an apartment together.

I'm sure there were other wives there, but I never saw much of them. They all spent their time at the officer's club or hung out at the pool, and that just wasn't my thing. I spent my time in the apartment cooking. I made all kinds of fabulous dinners, and whatever I made, Julie would say, "Never tasted anything so delicious!" To him, everything was so luscious, so I kept cooking more and more elaborate dinners. And every time, Julie would say, "Never have I tasted anything better! This is wonderful!"

At one point, Julie had a girlfriend, Lynn Gelfer, who wanted to visit him. They were both from Washington, D.C. Julie knew he was being transferred overseas, so he wanted to see Lynn before he left. Her mother refused to let her come.

"They're not engaged," Mrs. Gelfer said to me on the phone. "I can't have her going there without there being some kind of an understanding between them."

"Mrs. Gelfer, they'll never get engaged if you don't let her come," I said. "Besides, I'll be here, so they won't be alone."

Mrs. Gelfer let Lynn come after all, and of course they slept together. And just as I thought, they became engaged, got married, and had a lot of children.

Auden was invited to the University of Michigan at Ann Arbor to be a visiting professor for a year starting in the fall of 1941. He was asked to be one of the judges at the Hopwood awards which hosts a variety of contests and prizes for students at the University. Unfortunately, after reviewing all of the submissions, Auden declared that he "had not found a true poet in the lot."[88] He encouraged Chester to study at the university. He thought that Chester could earn a degree and submit his work in the Avery Hopwood competition. If he won, would he receive accolades and publication and win a good sum of money.[89] In the fall of 1941, Chester entered graduate school at the University of Michigan.

Auden had arranged for Chester to have a guest teaching spot at the University of Michigan, but Chester had other plans. As the weather grew colder, he decided that he would much rather vacation for a month in sunny Los Angeles, and per usual, he expected Auden to pay for everything. Although Europe had been at war since the Germans attacked Poland in 1939, the United States officially entered the war on December 7, 1941 when the Japanese bombed Pearl Harbor. On the day of the Japanese attack, Chester wrote to Auden and whined that war breaking out was ruining his Hollywood sex life. "It really isn't fair—I feel bitter, vindictive, half-immersed in 'circular madness…Is it asking so much to want to be fucked or even to indulge in the simplest of childhood experiences with a more dangerous engine??…it's all very depressing—and now War."[90] Auden was absolutely miserable. While Chester was off carousing with all the bronzed boys in California, on his dime no less, Auden was stuck in the cold Midwest surrounded by what he saw as simple, unsophisticated country folk.

While Auden suffered heartache and loneliness while Chester was living it up on the West Coast, my journey out west marked the beginning of my independent life. I felt free and happy and complete. You see, although I was with Morty, my relationship with him never made me feel as other wives might have felt at that time—as though they were playing the part of the dutiful wife, subordinate to their husbands lives and careers. With Morty, I was my own person. I was with him, not of him. It was the first time in my life that I had truly felt as though I was coming into my own.

After Morty's basic training in York, we drove out west to Spokane, WA. I was pregnant with twins at the time, and we stopped in Yellowstone to stay overnight in one of the cabins. As Morty unloaded the car, I went inside to lay down on the bed. Just as I closed my eyes, I heard strange footsteps.

"Morty? Is that you?"

He didn't answer, so I propped myself up on an elbow to take a look. I big black bear was standing in the doorway.

"Morty! Morty!"

Morty calmly walked in and kind of edged himself into the doorway right beside the bear.

"Shoo!" he said.

The bear turned around and walked out.

"That bear could have killed you."

"But he didn't."

And with that, Morty left the bedroom and resumed unpacking the car. The number of park rangers had been cut in half because of the war, so the bears were free to come into camp and scavenge for food as they pleased. They were as common in the campgrounds as the tourists. We were in Spokane only five days. I had just learned my way around the place when Morty was transferred to Pueblo, CO.

Chester had returned to Michigan after Christmas. From February to May 1942, Auden rented a Victorian house owned by Thomas A. Knott, the editor of *The Merriam-Webster Dictionary* while he and his wife took an extended vacation.[91] They were thrilled at the idea of having a poet in the house, believing that poets in particular had a sensitivity to beauty that no other arts possessed. The Knotts were very proud of their historic home with its pastel walls, hardwood floors, fancy chintz-upholstered furniture, and freshly painted kitchen. Mrs. Knott famously bragged that her floors were so clean that you could literally eat off of them. Unbeknownst to the Knotts, Auden and Chester had other ideas on how a household should be run.[92]

Auden and Chester moved in, and all hell broke loose. Their apartments always had the appearance of a condemned house set to be demolished by a wrecking ball. Chester, who was famous for cooking elaborate meals, always left the kitchen in shambles with the effect of having mixed food in a blender with the lid off. Once settled in the Knott's house, they invited guests over who spilled wine on rugs and left burning cigarettes to scorch the carpets, tables, furniture. Their hobnailed boots gouged the wooden floors. Dirty dishes stacked for weeks in the kitchen sink, on tables, on the floor, and even in the bath tub when it wasn't filled with cold water to chill bottles of champagne. If ever anyone tried to clean, Chester would "raise a wrist to his brow in a pained expression and say, 'Pul-eeze! Do not raise the dust!'" In a previous apartment, Auden left food out at night to feed a mouse. He did the same in the Knott's house in order to feed the rats that scurried into the house and settled in.[93]

When the Knotts returned, they were horrified to find that

their beautiful home was completely destroyed. The lovely hard-wood floors had been gashed by what looked like "dungeon chains." The walls were covered with ink, splashed food, and lipstick. The fancy kitchen curtains had been removed from their rods, used to wipe greasy hands, and tossed onto the back of a chair. The kitchen ceiling was splattered with what appeared to be tomato paste, but what could easily have been blood. They sued Auden for damages and won.[94]

Chapter Fourteen

The war in Europe raged on. When Auden left England for the United States in 1939, some considered him a traitor leaving his country in its hour of need. He came for a number of reasons, not one of them was to flee fascism. First, he left England eight months before the war broke out in a time when most thought that likelihood of war had been avoided. After war broke out, Auden contacted the British embassy in Washington, DC to let them know he was willing to go back and serve his country. They replied saying only qualified individuals were needed. When the United States entered the war, Auden was drafted in August 1942. He was again willing to fight but was dismissed because of his flat feet and poor eyesight.[95]

By February 1943, the bombing of Great Britain had begun. In occupied France, chilling photographs of famous writers tortured in concentration camps had been circulated in order to crush free speech. Other writers simply disappeared.[96] In the United States, rationing stamps were required to buy milk, cheese, canned goods, and butter. Shoes were rationed.[97]

My twins were due that June, however, one night in May I woke to find that I was covered in blood. It was 2:00 a.m., and I stumbled my way to the phone to call Morty. He was on duty at the Army base hospital. I stood in the hallway leaning against the wall as they ran to find him. After what seemed like an eternity, he finally picked up the phone.

"Morty, I'm bleeding. I'm standing in almost ankle-deep blood."

"Call Dr. Taylor and tell him that you have to go to the hospital. Then call the neighbor and tell him to take you to the hospital."

I thought to myself, you seriously want me to make all these telephone calls while I bleed to death in the hallway? He should have said, "Don't worry, I'll call the doctor and the neighbor." I think Morty must have read my mind and realized that I couldn't do any of those things, so he quickly came home and took me to the hospital.

When I got to St. Mary's Hospital, Dr. Taylor came and said,

"There has been a partial separation of the placenta, but one twin seems to be okay. We'll have to wait until morning to deliver the surviving baby."

I stayed in bed all night with Morty at my side and waited until sometime the following morning for the doctor to operate. I still wasn't in labor, but instead of inducing me, Dr. Taylor decided to do a C-Section. By then it was much too late. My sons, one weighing 5 pounds, the other weighing 5 pounds 2 ounces, died shortly after birth. If that wasn't bad enough, I developed a paralyzed intestine. It's called a paralytic ileus where the intestinal muscles become in-active preventing food to pass properly. It often occurs after a major surgery. The infection was so severe that at one point I almost died.

I found out many years later that Dr. Taylor was a drug addict. I got a letter from a friend in Colorado who said that Dr. Taylor had ODed on a street in Pueblo, CO. That's how everybody found out about his drug abuse. I also found out that when I came in to deliver my twins that night, Dr. Taylor had been too high to operate on me. There was no reason for me not to deliver right away except that he had to wait until morning in order to come down from his high.

Many years later, while living in Queens, we became friends with an obstetrician named Sid Druce. All my friends went to him, so I thought to myself, *why shouldn't I go to him, too, just because he's my friend?* The first time he examined me, he took one look at me and shook his head.

"What the hell was he trying to do, a tonsillectomy?"

Thanks to Dr. Taylor's handiwork, I now have a dreadful vertical incision the entire length of my abdomen.

Dr. Taylor's delay in delivering my babies reminds me of the story I read about Rosemary Kennedy. She was the sister of JFK whom the family never talked about. The infamous Spanish Flu of 1918-1919 had broken out in Boston in the Receiving Ship at Boston's Commonwealth Pier on August 28, 1918. Within a week, two dozen sailors were sickened. By mid-September, the flu had spread to nearly 2,000 soldiers at the shipyard. The hospitals overflowed with infected patients, so a hospital tent was erected in nearby Brookline, MA to care for the sick.

On September 13, 1918 in Brookline, MA, Rose Kennedy went into labor with her third child. Dr. Good was called to drive out to the Kennedy home to deliver the baby, but he was in the midst of treating the many flu patients. The nurse had been trained to deliver the baby, but she was instructed to wait for the doctor. Instead of allowing the baby to be born naturally, they delayed the birth two hours in order for the doctor to arrive. The nurse held Rose's legs together, and at one point, she reached up into Rose's birth canal and held the baby's head in place. Preventing a baby to move through the birth canal can deprive it of oxygen which could cause brain damage.[98]

Dr. Good finally arrived and delivered what appeared to be a normal, healthy baby girl. Later on, it became clear that something was wrong with Rosemary. She struggled in school and wasn't as active as her siblings. She was angry and confused and sometimes had fits which might have been seizures. Rosemary often ran away.

Rose took Rosemary to see a doctor who diagnosed her as mentally retarded having suffered a "uterine accident." At that time, mental illness wasn't something a family discussed. Joe Sr. had been honing his two eldest sons for political life. A mentally retarded sibling could have spelled disaster for a budding career in the spotlight. So, upon the advice of Dr. Walter Freeman and Dr. James Watts, and despite objections from the family, Rosemary underwent a prefrontal lobotomy. Dr. Freeman, who often hammered ice picks up through the eye sockets, inserted a small metal spatula into Rosemary's brain and sliced the connections between her pre-frontal cortex and the rest of her brain.

After the lobotomy, Rosemary was unable to walk or talk. She was sent to live at Craig House, a psychiatric facility where Zelda Fitzgerald once stayed. It would be twenty years until Rosemary saw the rest of the family.[99]

After Joe Kennedy's death in 1969, Rosemary was occasionally taken to visit her family. She was able to walk with a limp, but her arms shook terribly, and she wasn't able to speak. Rosemary's condition wasn't exactly what inspired Eunice Kennedy Shrive to found the Special Olympics, but she confessed that if she hadn't known or loved Rosemary, she might not have been exposed to anyone with mental and physical handicaps because back then, people kept those conditions secret.[100]

If that nurse hadn't held Rose Kennedy's legs together, Rosemary might have been born healthy and lived a normal life. And if Dr. Taylor hadn't been high when I was rushed to the hospital, I could have delivered my sons on time. I have no doubt that one if not both of them would have survived. The grief of their loss may have faded, but their death is scar on my heart I will live with forever. If their lives hadn't been snuffed out, what would they have accomplished, invented, inspired? I can't help but wonder what incredible men they would have been.

Chapter Fifteen

T he war shoved on. From 1939 to 1940, a majority of all immigration to the United States were Jews fleeing from the Nazis throughout Europe. The State Department received information regarding widespread atrocities and reports of Jewish genocide. Either they couldn't believe the horrific accounts or they turned a blind eye. Whatever the reason, the reports were considered to be outrageous rumors, so the information was never forwarded.

Many newspapers in the Unites States at the time weren't really covering the horrors that were happening to the Jews. They mentioned shootings and mass murder, but they often didn't specify who the victims were. It wasn't until the finals days of the war when the concentration camps were being liberated that the world learned the full scope of Hitler's horrors.[101]

To tell you the truth, Morty and I weren't too concerned with what was happening overseas. We were living on the Army base in Pueblo, Colorado—in the mountains. Tragically, airplanes would try to land at the base, but would often crash into the mountainside. It was horrible. Many people died. Things may have been happening overseas, but our focus was on whatever was happening in our own back yard.

We were the only Jews on the base, and Morty was the only Jew-ish doctor. After a few years, another Jewish doctor, Dr. Koch, was assigned to the base, and he brought his wife, Hilda. My friends on the base commented to me about this other Jewish couple.

"Now, they're from New York, but they're not like you," my good friend, Alfreda, said. "They're cheap and loud and brash and very showy."

"So, what you're saying is that we're white Jews. But really, it doesn't have anything to do with being Jewish. Look at Roy Porter. He's a skinflint, and he's an Episcopalian."

Alfreda was the commanding officer's wife. I know that Morty had been given orders to go overseas, but she told her husband, "Nope. We can't let that happen. We have to keep him here." Morty was on limited service because of his poor eyesight, so he had a good excuse to remain in the United States. Even so, it was nice of her to insist that we stay.

I was very young at the time, but Alfreda told me that I had taught her so much about the nature of people who were different.

"Before I met you and got to know you," she said, "I would have crossed the street to avoid you."

"I confess, I might have crossed the street to avoid you, too, and yet, here we are good friends."

Narrow-mindedness is simply fear-based prejudice passed on from one generation to the next like a bad gene. It takes education, exposure, and courage to change one's mind about someone. It might not be easy, but it certainly can be done.

In July of 1944, my son, Steven, was born at St. Mary's Hospi-tal in Pueblo, CO. The thing that was so dumb was that even after everything that went wrong with my twins' delivery, when I got pregnant again, I went back to Dr. Taylor. I had no idea about his drug abuse, and I trusted that what he said and did at the time was the proper treatment.

Shortly after Steven was born, I developed childbed fever or puerperal sepsis. It's a bacterial infection of the reproductive tract that comes on quite suddenly. It begins with intense shivering, then progresses to a high fever and severe, sometimes unbearable abdominal pain. At one point, it accounted for nearly half of all childbirth deaths.[102] Childbed fever was so common that it was customary for a doctor or midwife to announce that the mother was the one who had been delivered and not the baby.[103] Even today, Buckingham Palace places a placard announcing a royal birth by saying that the mother, for example The Duchess of Cambridge, was safely delivered of a son.

I was in extreme pain and delirious with a very high fever. They placed me in an oxygen tank, and in those days, the tanks were big brown canvas tents that had a small Plexiglas window toward the top. A tiny bit of light bled through, but the angle was so high that you couldn't see out. When I came to, I thought for sure that I was at the bottom of a grave and had been buried alive. I began to scream. I ripped out all of the tubes and pipes and pushed my way out of the tent. I slid off the bed and wandered into the hallway. I headed toward the nurse's desk at the end of the corridor. I had it in my mind that I had to call Morty and tell him to come and get me out of there.

As I walked down the corridor, I noticed that there were patient rooms on either side of the hall all the way down the corridor. I thought to myself, *if a nurse should come, I'll go into one of the patient rooms and ask them to hide me under the bed.* I remember thinking this so clearly. But no nurse came. I made it to the end of the hallway to the nurse's desk, and no one was on duty. I picked up the phone, asked the operator to dial a number, and my mother answered the phone.

"Let me speak to Morty."

Morty got on the phone, and I said, "You have to come and get me right away. Dr. Taylor is coming, and he's going to put all these tubes back into my body."

"Where are you?"

"Where do you think I am? I'm in the hospital."

"I know that. Where are you exactly?"

"I'm at the nurse's desk."

Just then, everybody came—nurses, doctors, everybody—and they hauled me back to my room. They placed a nun in my room for the rest of the night to sit right beside my bed as though I was under house arrest. They said it was to keep me company, but I knew she was really there to make sure I didn't escape.

"Now, when Dr. Taylor comes back," the nurse said, "he's going to put your IVs back in."

The interesting thing about this whole episode was that there had been a terrible storm that night. Morty had tried to call the hospital, but the wires were all down, so he couldn't get through. But somehow, my telephone call went through. And years later, I thought, could I have imagined all that? There was no way I could have made that phone call. It was impossible. However, I know it happened, because my mother answered the phone, and Morty spoke to me.

It was a busy hospital with people constantly bustling around. So, why weren't there any nurses or doctors in the hallway that night? I wasn't at all well, so I certainly wasn't running down the hall. It took a very long time for me to drag myself along the hallway. And not only that, after I made it to the empty nurse's station, I picked up the receiver and gave my number to the operator. She never asked, "Who is this?"

The whole thing is very strange, and it has always fascinated me. To this day, I can't explain it. Albert Einstein once said that,

"Imagination is more important than knowledge. For knowledge is limited to all we now know and understand, while imagination embraces the entire world, and all there ever will be to know and understand." I was so desperate, and my need to get in touch with Morty and have him get me out of that hospital was so urgent that somehow my thoughts manifested all that went on that night. I'm sure of it. Whenever I hear someone say the expression, "Stranger things have happened," I think to myself, yep, they sure have.

Chapter Sixteen

The spring of 1944 melted into summer, and the Soviets advanced on the concentration camps in Poland. By January 1945, they liberated the largest and most vile of killing machines, Auschwitz. As the U.S. and British forces joined the Soviets in liberating more and more camps, the Germans tried burning their death camps in order to depose of any evidence of the mass murders before they fled. Some of the buildings may have burned, but the crematoriums remained intact.[104]

On April 12, 1945, FDR had been at his retreat home in Warm Springs, GA dubbed the Little White House. He often traveled there hoping to find a cure for his infantile paralysis. That afternoon, FDR sat in this living room with Lucy Mercer, with whom he had an affair, his two cousins and his dog, Fala, while the artist, Elizabeth Shoumatoff, painted his portrait. At about 1 p.m., FDR suddenly grabbed the back of his head.

"I have a terrific pain in the back of my head."

He immediately slumped forward in his chair and was carried unconscious to his bedroom. Although his cardiologist, Howard Bruenn, gave him a shot of adrenaline to the heart, there was no way to revive him. The president was pronounced dead of a massive cerebral hemorrhage at 3:35 p.m.[105]

Eleanor Roosevelt had been at a piano recital in Washington, D.C. after a speech she had given when she was summoned back to the White House. She wrote later in her memoirs that while riding back to the White House, she knew in her bones that her husband was dead. Once she arrived, aides told her what she already knew. She and her daughter, Anna, donned black dresses, and after she phoned her sons, Eleanor broke the news to Vice President Harry Truman.

"Harry, the president is dead," Eleanor said calmly.

"Is there anything I can do for you?" he asked.

"Is there anything we can do for *you*? For you are the one in trouble now."

FDR was a tough act to follow. He had served four extraordinary terms—the longest tenure in American history. He had seen this country out of the Great Depression and steered us through most of WWII. Amazingly, FDR had kept Truman completely in the dark about the development of the atomic bomb. It was only after his death that Truman learned about the Manhattan Project.[106] After getting up to speed, it was then up to him if his new weapon would be used.

That same month, with the Nazis negotiating their surrender in Milan and the anti-fascists advancing from the north, 61-year-old Mussolini realized that his power had vanished. He donned a disguise and fled toward Lake Como with his 33-year-old girlfriend, Clara Petacci, in order to escape over the Swiss border. Since his face had been arrogantly plastered on propaganda posters and press slogans, partisans quickly recognized him. He and Clara were seized, and the following day, April 28, 1945, they were ordered to stand against a stone wall where they were executed by machine gunfire.

Just before the sun rose on April 29th, their bodies along with 14 others fascists were tossed from a truck in Milan's town square Piazzale Loreto. People screamed insults, threw rotten vegetables, kicked, and spat upon the corpses. One woman took a pistol and shot five rounds into Mussolini's dead body declaring, "Five shots for my five assassinated sons!" The crowd then strung up the bodies by their feet. After they were taken down by American troops, in a final act of humiliation, someone posed Mussolini and Clara's bodies side by side as though the lovers were nestled together.[107]

On that same day, Hitler married his longtime mistress, Eva Braun, in a secret ceremony. The following day, he had lunch as usual at 2:00 p.m., and shortly after 3:00 p.m., he poisoned his most cherished dog, Blondi, and all her pups. He and Eva Hitler retreated to an air-raid bunker where they sat together on their sofa and both bit into glass vials of cyanide. As he did this, Hitler took out his 7.65 mm Walther pistol and shot himself in the head. While Hitler remained in an upright sitting position in death, Eva curled up on the sofa beside him and waited for the poison to take her.

Hamburg Radio reported the following day that Hitler had died bravely fighting for the Third Reich until his very last breath.[108] In truth, he was a coward in life and a coward in death. He was never remorseful for any of the suffering he had caused his victims, nor the pain he had inflicted on the world with his war. He died a pathetic little man in the ground, no better than vermin.

I must have had family in Europe who suffered during the Holocaust. I know I have relatives on both my mother's and father's sides of the family who never left Russia, so it's very possible that my family members were sent to concentration camps and either died or were liberated. For all I know, they could have all perished in the Holocaust. Sadly, I just don't know.

Shortly after Hitler committed suicide, V-E Day or Victory in Europe Day on May 8th signaled the unconditional surrender of all German forces. Although the world cheered the end of the war, fighting wasn't quite over. Battles were still being waged in Burma, Singapore, the Philippines, New Guinea, Thailand, and Okinawa. Kamikazes were still flying their planes into Allied ships.

I remember I was in my kitchen on August 6, 1945. Steven had just learned to crawl. I was standing in my kitchen looking down at Steven playing on the floor banging on the pots and pans with a wooden spoon. I can remember that moment so very clearly. Every ghastly detail is frozen in my mind. I had the radio on and was listening to music as I cooked dinner when a news flash broke in. President Harry Truman announced that we had dropped the atom bomb on Hiroshima, Japan:

"A short time ago, an American airplane dropped one bomb on Hiroshima and destroyed its usefulness to the enemy. That bomb had more power than 20,000 tons of TNT. The Japanese began the war from the air at Pearl Harbor. They have been repaid many fold. And the end is not yet. With this bomb, we have now added a new and revolutionary increase in destruction to supplement the growing power of our armed forces. In their present form, these bombs are now in production and even more powerful forms are in development. It is an atomic bomb. It is a harnessing of the basic power of the universe. The force from which the sun draws its power has been loosed against those who brought war to the Far East."

"We are now prepared to destroy more rapidly and completely every productive enterprise the Japanese have in any city. We shall destroy their docks, their factories, and their communications. Let there be no mistake; we shall completely destroy Japan's power to make war."[109]

Truman went on to suggest that the United States was the greatest nation in the world and from then on, we were going to see to it that there was peace—our way. I sat down at the table and wept. I sobbed for those poor people and out of the utter humiliation I felt toward our ignorant leader—to hear that man arrogantly say that we were greatest nation on earth because we annihilated all those innocent men, women, and children.

It was so horrifying! And yet, my brother-in-law, Bernie Stowens, who was a physicist, said, "It was the best thing that happened, because it shortened the war." That simply wasn't true, because the Japanese were already talking about peace. Their pilots were desperately signing up for Kamikaze suicide missions and flying into our aircraft carriers for goodness sake. They were at the end of their rope.

Those bombs didn't have to be dropped, except that Truman had to show himself to be some big shot. Well, let me tell you, he was a little man who had to compensate for his small stature and his meager manhood. Oh, how I hated that man! He succeeded FDR, who was a tough act to follow. So, he had to show that he was important. And that's what he did. He killed hundreds of thousands of people. When you think of it, it's mind boggling. Alan Turing cracking the Enigma Code shortened the war by several years. It was so crucial that Winston Churchill said that Turing made the single biggest contribution to Allied victory. By peacefully ending the war early, he actually *saved* millions of lives. He was brilliant and strategic. Harry Truman was nothing more than an impotent little man.

Years later, Morty and I were at a conference in Italy and we took a day-trip to sites all around Florence. We befriended two Japanese women on the bus. As we ate lunch together, I couldn't help but ask them, "It must be so difficult for you to be around us—to deal with Americans."

"Yes, it is," one of them said.

The subject never came up between us again, but I couldn't help feeling ashamed for what our government had done. Every time I see Trump, I think of Truman. In fact, in 2017, Trump gave a saber-rattling speech about North Korea:

"North Korea best not make any more threats to the United States. They will be met with fire and fury like the world has never seen. They will be met with fire, fury, and frankly power the likes of which this world has never seen before."[110]

The likes of which have never been seen. The same words Truman used after he bombed Japan. I picture Trump with his small finger on that bomb. If he decides to bomb a country for whatever reason, and he'll find a reason, nobody can stop him. Someone told me that he can be stopped, but I don't think so. I know Congress is the one who decides if the president can declare war, so in theory, the president can't go to war without their approval. That said, when General John "Mick" Nicholson, the top U.S. commander in Afghanistan, decided to drop the largest non-nuclear bomb nicknamed the "Mother of all Bombs" on a system of ISIS tunnels in Afghanistan, he didn't ask permission. Apparently, he didn't have to."[111] We've been in a war in Afghanistan for 16 years, and nobody declared war. On September 14, 2001, Congress handed the reigns over to President Bush to declare war stating that he could fight any "nations, organizations, or persons that he believes had a hand in the 9/11 terror attacks, or any nation who harbors such terrorists." Unfortunately, that resolution doesn't name any particular country or set any military goals for when we go in, or where we go in, or what we do exactly once we get in, or how long we do it—whatever "it" is, or when we decide to get out. Once President Bush got that blank check from Congress, forget Afghanistan. He set his sights on the Philippines, Iraq, Somalia, Sudan, Yemen, Syria, and Indonesia. That resolution gave him "absolute, dictatorial power to wage lasting war, world war, or nuclear war."[112] So, where is Congress when we need them? And when does this madness end?

Like Trump did in the campaign when he thought he might lose the election, he whips his followers, his base, into a frenzy. His followers are with him through thick and thin. Look, if they didn't immediately drop him after the Mexican rapist remarks, or the grabbing of the crotch bluster, or the making fun of the disabled display, and all his other shenanigans, then they never will. He goes out to these rallies now and riles up his base as though he's still campaigning.

The thing that scares me is that, once cornered, Trump will foment a revolt. When he sees his presidency failing, and he can't help but see it, he goes out on the "trail" and throws red meat to his base. And they eat it up. You see them at their rallies screaming and pumping their fists in the air—that mob mentality. It's very frightening. All those crazies are following a lunatic. Just where will that lead us? I recently read an article that said the Televangelist, Jim Bakker, is calling on all Christians to arms in the event of Trump's impeachment.

"If it happens, there will be a civil war in the United States of America. The Christians will finally come out of the shadows, because we are going to be shut up permanently if we're not careful."[113]

We're living through some crazy times. I pray that enough civic leaders and those at the helms of the churches, temples, and mosques have cooler heads, and that good judgment and sanity will prevail. I'd like to believe that, but I'm afraid at this point, I feel hopeless.

Tania Kurella Stern and W. H. Auden,
Washington DC, March 1945

Stern, James (1904-93) / Private Collection /
© James & Tania Stern Literary Estate / Bridgeman Images

Chapter Seventeen

On March 29, 1945, it was announced that Auden was to be given the Award of Merit Medal in Literature for poetry from the American Academy of Arts and Letters. He missed the award ceremony in May, because he and several hundred civilians traveled to Nuremberg, Germany after the war with the Morale Division of the U.S. Strategic Bombing Survey (USSBS). Their objective was to gather information from those German people who had been bombed by the allies and whose life as they knew it was over. The people interviewed were divided into groups from towns that had not been bombed at all to those towns that had been lightly bombed to those whose towns had been completely destroyed.[114]

Auden was embarrassed and repulsed by the types of questions the Morale Division required him to ask those poor people, for example, "What it was liked to be bombed?" They traveled to cities that had been completely leveled, and he was required to ask the ludicrous question, "To your knowledge, did any bombs drop on your city?"

You know the expression: ask a stupid question, get a stupid answer. To those people, Auden must have appeared to have been

a complete ignoramus. Auden wrote that those poor people trying to live in those ruined cities were "sad beyond belief." By the
time he was finished with his duties, he had written to a composer
friend, Nicolas Nabokov, about his experience saying, "I know that
[the Germans] had *asked* for it, but this kind of total destruction
is beyond reasoning…It's absolutely ghastly…is it justified to reply to *their* mass-murder by *our* mass-murder? It seems terrifying
to me."[115]

Auden returned to New York that autumn and taught at The New
School, Bennington College, Smith College, and other institutions
throughout the United States. It was about this time in 1945 that
the February House at 7 Middagh Street was emptied, and the rows
of townhouses were bulldozed to make way for the Brooklyn-Queens
Expressway. Now where the houses with all their ghosts once stood,
a chain link fence rambles along the bluff that overlooks the traffic
churning in and out of the city. Hooked onto the fence is a sign that
reads "No Standing Anytime."

Auden and Chester settled into an apartment at 7 Cornelia Street
in Greenwich Village. It was a cozy place despite the almost unbeliev-
able messiness and the permanent smell of cat piss. From then on,
Auden had a cat in his life. This particular cat, it's safe to say, took
over the apartment. Whenever dinner guests came by, the cat jumped
up and sashayed across the table, sniffed the plates, sampled the food,
and flicked his tail across the salad bowl.[116]

On May 20, 1946, Auden officially became a United States cit-
izen. He often said that his relationship with Chester was a driving
force in his decision.[117] Once he officially became an American citi-
zen, he was no longer eligible to be appointed Poet Laureate in England. Nevertheless, because he was so famous and popular, he was
granted the title anyway.

It was a sweet time for Auden. He had settled into his platonic, domestic life with Chester, and they seemed happy with their new arrangement. In addition to all the dinner parties the two of them hosted, Auden began the tradition of having champagne parties on February 21st to celebrate his birthday. He sent out invitations saying 'Carriages at one,' which was a polite way of saying, 'The party will wrap up by 1 o'clock, so everybody needs to go home then.' These soirees soon became *the* place to be seen within the New York Literary circle.[118]

Each summer, Auden and Chester escaped the city heat to party and relax on Fire Island with the rest of the sophisticated homosexual crowd. In the summer of 1947, a lavish carnival was held where Auden came dressed as a bishop with miter, cope, and all. Chester came dressed as a very "rococo angel."[119]

Chester Kallman in drag.[120]

It was a sweet time in our lives as well. Morty had been transferred to Colorado Springs, and we settled into our new life there. I
remember sitting on the sofa with Steven once with an animal picture book on our laps. He was about two years old at the time. I
would point to the picture of the dog and say "Dog," and he'd say
"Dog." I would point to the picture of the cat and say, "Cat." He'd
repeat, "Cat." "Cow," ... "Cow." "Squirrel," ... "Fuck." I would repeat, "Squirrel," and he would repeat, "Fuck." I would say to Steven
slowly, "Squii-rrel," and he would repeat slowly, "Fu-uuck." I have
absolutely no idea why. Everyone insisted that I taught him that. Julie and Lynn came to visit, and he would say, "Steven, say Uncle Julie
Squirrel," and they'd all howl with laughter when Steven said "Fuck."

Many years later, Steven was married and living in Colorado,
and he was invited to speak at the Smithsonian. So, I asked Lynn
and Julie to meet us there and hear Steven speak. Afterwards, we all
went out to dinner with Steven's colleagues. Julie was a doctor by this
time, too, but the first thing he said to Steven at dinner was, "Steven,
say squirrel."

In 1945, Morty had finished his service in the Army. We decided to move back to New York. Little did we know that as soon as
Morty and I had left New York for the Army, my father had rented
our house out without telling us and kept the money. We couldn't
have lived in our house all year round at that time anyway, because
there was no heat and no insulation. It was meant to be more of a
summer home. Besides, by that time we had one-year-old Steven.
That was beside that point. It was wrong of my father to rent our
house without telling us and then keep the money. He could have at
least given us a share of the money, but he kept every last dime. That
was my father.

One night, we went to dinner with a married couple, Muriel and
Dave Dulberg, that we met while stationed in Colorado Springs.

"We just bought a house in Flushing, Queens," Muriel said.

"Really?" I asked. "Why Queens? Who lives in Queens?"

"We do! We put $500 down, and we were able to buy a lovely house. You should come by the neighborhood and see it."

So, right after dinner, we drove out to Flushing, Queens and looked at their house. And it looked like a real house, except that it was attached to other houses. I later learned that these were townhouses. It had two stories, three bedrooms, and two baths.

"Where are the windows?" I asked.

"They're in the front and the back."

"But where are the other windows?"

"Well, we have no other windows. The house is attached on either side."

I couldn't picture what that was like, and I was living in a brownstone. Go figure.

"Would you mind if our cousin George comes out to see the house?"

"Of course, he can come by.'

The next day, George, who designed our summer home in Mohegan, came out and took a look at the house.

"They're asking $10,000 for these houses," Morty said as we followed George through the house. "We'd pay $500 down and then so much a month. What do you think?"

"I think it's a good deal. Take it."

Of course, just coming home from the Army, we didn't have $500 at the time, so Morty asked his mother if we could borrow the money from her.

"You know, $500 is a lot of money," Lena said.

"Yes, it is," Morty said. "We'll pay you back as soon as possible."

"You most certainly will, and with interest."

With interest. I wasn't surprised.

We bought the house in 1947 and settled in. I remember Steven had a best friend named Bobby Block who was also about three years old. Bobby often came over to the house to play. One time, they were at the kitchen table eating lunch, and I asked Bobby if he wanted some more milk.

"Wes, please," Bobby said.

Obviously, Bobby was a little Dutchie and couldn't say his Ys.

Steven laughed and laughed and said, "Bobby says 'Wes.' That's because he's too yiddle to say yes."

Steven couldn't say his Ls. Years later, both of his daughters couldn't pronounce Fs. Whenever we visited them in Colorado, Morty, who always carried a lot of pens in his shirt pocket, would say to the girls, "One, Two, Three," and Elizabeth would say, "Bour, Bibe, Six." They both had that same Dutchieness, but they grew out of it as I knew Steven would when he was older.

In 1947, I became pregnant again. Morty and I sat down with Steven and explained to him that he was going to have a baby brother or baby sister. That June, our son, Dan, was born. I had been so sick when Steven was born that I never had the chance to really enjoy holding my newborn baby. There's something about the smell of a newborn baby's head that is incredibly soothing. I swear, if warring people could just lay down their weapons for one minute and smell a baby's head, there would be world peace.

When Morty brought Steven to the hospital to see me and meet the baby, Steven took one look at Dan and made a face.

"What do we need him for?" Steven said.

Despite that inauspicious beginning, Steven took Dan under his wing. I remember watching the boys play out the window. At that time, the street we lived on was very quiet. The new townhouses had been built on top of a swamp that had been drained. They had been constructed quickly for those veterans returning home from the war.

I watched as Steven ran across the road to fetch a ball. Dan toddled into the street after him. Steven spun around and yelled at Dan.

"How many times do I have to tell you, you gotta run faster. You're my responsibility."

One evening, after I finished reading to the boys, Steven looked perplexed.

"What's the matter," I asked. "Didn't you like the story?"

"I was thinking," Steven said. "What are the advantages of being older?"

"Well, you get to go to bed 15 minutes later," I said.

"What about me?" Dan asked. "What are my advantages?"

I didn't have the heart to tell him that he would always be the baby in my eyes. Before I could say anything, he chimed in.

"Oh, I know. I'll die three years later than Steven will."

My boys were so clever and had always seemed older and wiser than their years. For example, I've never been a morning person. Even nowadays, people know not to call me before 11 a.m. When Dan and Steven were very young, they signed a petition for me not to come downstairs in the morning. Ha!

After the boys were born, we decided to add several rooms onto the Mohegan house. Morty was going to use one or two of the extra rooms and set up his medical practice there. He talked to the doctors in Peekskill about a possible partnership but got nowhere.

"Look," one of the doctors told him, "we have enough pediatricians here. We certainly don't need another one."

It was their way of saying "thanks, but no thanks," so, Morty gave that idea up.

The following year, we bought another, bigger house in Queens on a corner with a finished basement and separate entrance where Morty kept his office. When we put our first house up for sale, for $12,000, a man came out to take a look. I followed him through the house as he went room by room.

He stamped his foot on the floor. "The floors are weak," he said. He pounded his hands against the walls. "The walls are very shaky. How much do you want?"

"We put in the paper that we wanted $12,000."

"That's what you're asking. What do you want?"

"If we didn't want $12,000, we wouldn't have asked for $12,000."

This is how much I knew about selling a house. I had no idea I was expected to haggle.

"Come to think of it," I said, "I don't think you'll be happy in this house. After all, the floors are no good, and the walls are no good. It's not a good idea for you to buy this house. Goodbye."

We eventually got a buyer at $12,000, so it worked out in the end.

When Dan was very little, he learned to play the violin. He has perfect pitch. I'm tone deaf, and he has perfect pitch. Go figure. Anyway, he came home one time after one of his first lessons.

"Would you like to hear me play something?" he asked.

"Of course," I said. "What can you play?"

"Well, I can play a C and an E. Which would you like to hear first?"

Our sons brought us such joy, and Morty and I were happy. Morty began specializing in care of the mentally retarded children. We weren't rich by any stretch of the imagination, but for the first time, thanks to Morty's practice, we were able to really enjoy life. We traveled, went to the theater, and invited friends over to the house for cocktails and dinner parties. Everything in our lives seemed perfect.

Then the accident happened.

Chapter Eighteen

One evening in September 1947, my mother's brother, Albert Halprin, was driving back to the Colony from the city with his son, my cousin Ben Halprin, who had saved me from marrying Ben Barison, his sister Anne Elizabeth, who we all called "Sister Halprin," and our uncle Phil Fried, one of the founders of the Colony. They had been to the city to pay a condolence call and were driving north on the Palisades Parkway. A drunk driver, the brother of a big shot Hollywood producer, was driving the wrong direction on their side of the highway and plowed into them. As is often the case, the drunk driver lived, and all of my family died.

It was so traumatic for our family. From that day forward, everything is dated from the accident. We mark time as things that happened before or after the accident—like BC and AD.

A huge trial ensued. Instead of jail time, the drunken man's lawyers argued that he should remain free in order to make lots of money for Ben's wife, Eleanor, and their six-month-old baby girl. I wanted them to lock him up and throw away the key.

Ben and Ellie had just built a big beautiful house in the Colony, but instead of living in the house without Ben, she decided to move in with Aunt Mary, Albert's wife. People grieve in their own way. Some look for solitude, while others need the company of others to work through their sorrow. I suppose Ellie thought that it would make all of their grief easier to bear if they carried the burden together.

After every dark day, the sun rises and life must go on. Morty's practice flourished and the boys did well in school. We took the boys to concerts and plays and museums. One time, we took Dan to the Museum of Natural History when he was a small boy. He was so afraid of the dinosaurs!

"There's no need to be frightened," I said. "All these animals are dead."

"Then why aren't they laying down?"

We dressed them up for Halloween and cooked turkey for Thanksgiving. Come December, we celebrated Christmas and Hanukkah by putting up both a Christmas tree and a Menorah. I love Christmas. It's such a cozy holiday with baking cookies and singing carols. Rockefeller Center officially started the tradition of putting up a Christmas tree in 1933 the same year 30 Rockefeller Plaza opened. The skating rink below was opened in 1936. And no holiday in New York would be complete without strolling the streets and taking in the festive department store window displays. In the late 1800s, plate glass windows were commonly placed in the front of the stores, and elaborate decorations were created to lure customers into the store—and "window shopping" was born.[121]

I loved decorating the tree. The Christmas tree was popular in the 17th century in Germany, but the tradition that we're most familiar with today took off when the German Prince Albert, husband of Queen Victoria, decorated a large evergreen tree in Windsor Castle at Christmastime in 1841.[122] But the tradition of bringing in evergreen boughs in midwinter predates Christianity as a way of celebrating the winter solstice.

When the boys were little, we would invite a few guests over to the house to help us decorate the tree. I served cocktails and a few hors d'oeuvres. It seemed with each passing year, the guest list grew, and the entertaining became more elaborate. Eventually, I began making a huge holiday sandwich from a gigantic round peasant loaf cut horizontally creating two open-faced sandwiches. First, I would spread both with seasoned butter just to hold what went on it. Then in the center of each, I would spoon on dollops of caviar, surround that with a piping of cream cheese, layer slices of smoked salmon. Around the edge, I placed green and red olives then sliced it up like a pie. We eventually had to stop when the guest list topped seventy people!

And I continued to write. Here's a poem I wrote in 1949 called *Two Symbols*. I've been asked what my inspiration was, but I can't really tell you.

1949

Two Symbols

Two symbols they
Of confused humanity
Ever seeking
Immortality
Searching always
For the right
Blindly groping
Toward unseen sight
Witless, dumb,
Led by each breeze
To bend and moan

Till, broke with ease
Their plodding minds
Realized no foe,
Their eyelids raised
On tearless woe.

                    While it is men
                    Who labor yet
                    Their women weep
                    To pay the debt
                    Incurred by thieves
                    Who work in pairs
                    To cheat dead Life
                    Of life's despairs.

They woke and slept
To sound of bells
Which were not heard
In conscious cells.
Their tuneless ears
Heard only groans
A race apart
These subway drones.
They never saw the starlit night
Without the bars
Of defined fright
Their present fear
Did bind their life
And force their hearts
To constant strife

Oh, it is men
Who don't regret
While women weep
To pay the debt
Incurred by thieves
Who work in pairs
To cheat dead Life
Of life's despairs.

How long can they
With heart and mind
Live without joy
No hope to find?
When will the dam
That burdens sight
Burst with a roar?
Let in the light?
Why do we think
who fasten the plow
It e'er will hold
Jailed force in tow?
Theirs is the might
Who now are thronged
And theirs the right
Who now are wronged.

While it is men
Who labor yet
Their women weep
To pay the debt
Incurred by thieves

Who work in pairs
To cheat dead Life
Of life's despairs.

I like to observe people, reflect on our shared struggles, and pon-der over why we're here. The meaning of life is different for differ-ent people. For some, life is about love. Aristotle believed that life was about happiness, and that happiness is the entire aspiration for human existence. Still for others, it's a way of working through the lessons our souls need to learn in order to progress to a higher state. I certainly don't have the answers, so I prefer to accept that I don't know and stay open-minded to all the possibilities.

Chapter Nineteen

In October of 1947, the composer Igor Stravinsky wrote to Auden saying he was composing a full-length opera in English called *The Rake's Progress,* and he wanted Auden to write the libretto. In typical Auden fashion, he replied immediately writing, "DELIGHTED." Stravinsky then wrote back inviting him to visit and stay with him and his wife in Hollywood.

Auden arrived at their house in mid-November carrying a small bag and a huge cow-skin rug, a gift to Stravinsky from one of Auden's friends in Argentina. The Stravinskys later described Auden as a big, blond intellectual bloodhound. He slept with his body on the couch and his feet covered by a blanket tethered down with books on a nearby chair.[123]

Back in New York, Auden immediately began to write the libretto. Without Stravinsky's permission, Auden asked Chester to collaborate with him. It was only after he mailed Act I to Stravinsky that he confessed that he had taken on a collaborator— "an old friend of mine in whose talents I have the greatest confidence." Auden assured him that Chester was just as good a librettist as he was, maybe even better. Stravinsky was not happy but agreed to trust Auden and wrote back saying he looked forward to meeting Chester in New York.

Stravinsky read the entire libretto and was pleasantly surprised."[124]

Stravinsky had hoped to have had the premiere in the United States as it was to be performed in English, but instead, it was first shown at the Teatro La Fenice in Venice, Italy.

W.H. Auden and Chester Kallman at home
on Ischia, Italy early 1950s.
(Photo by The John Deakin Archive/Getty Images)

Auden and Chester began to spend their summers on the island of Ischia, Italy, returning every year. He loved that island and even wrote a poem titled *Ischia* as a thank you to the place.

> Dearest to each his birthplace; but to recall a green
> Valley where mushrooms fatten in the summer nights
> And silvered willows copy the circumflexions of the stream
> Is not my gladness today; I am presently moved
> By sun—drenched Parthenopea, my thanks are for you,
> Ischia, to whom a fair wind has
> Brought me rejoicing with dear friends
> From soiled productive cities. How well you correct
> Our injured eyes, how gently you train us to see
> Things and men in perspective
> Underneath your uniform light. (lines 12-22)[125]

Their time on Ischia was blessed, but as the author J. K. Ensley said, "Every curse has a blessing and every blessing has a curse." Just before one of his summer trips in 1951, Auden flew from New York to London in May to visit with Stephen Spender before heading to Ischia. He had been an acquaintance of a man named Guy Burgess since the 1930s. Burgess, a flamboyant homosexual, telephoned Auden at Spender's house. Spender told the man that Auden was out. Burgess had been anxious to speak with Auden presumably to stay at his house in Ischia. Spender took the message, but for some reason, never gave it to Auden.

The following day, on May 25th, Guy Burgess and Donald Maclean fled England and defected to Moscow. It turned out Burgess and Maclean were British spies. That Monday, May 28th, Auden flew to Ischia and was met by the Italian police. Apparently, MI5 had been watching Auden for years, describing him as "an intellectual communist of a highly-idealistic and literary brand."[126] They were frustrated at not being able to interview Auden as he remained holed up in his Ischia home. Newspaper reporters and plainclothes policemen staked out his house day and night. To make matters worse, even though Auden didn't know Guy very well, a media frenzy ensued. The Italian press wrote a scathing exposé suggesting that Auden was also a spy in cahoots with Burgess, and that he helped Burgess and Maclean to escape. They also suggested that Auden was a Communist. Auden denied everything.

The upcoming premiere of *The Rake's Progress* would take Auden's mind off his troubles.[127] He and Chester were very excited to travel to Venice. Auden admired Stravinsky greatly. In fact, someone asked if he'd ever collaborate with the composer again. Auden replied that "being asked to work with Stravinsky was the greatest honour he had ever received."[128]

Just as they were about to depart for Venice, Chester asked Auden if he would mind if he brought his lover. Chester had been seeing a boy named Alessandro for a few summers. In Italy at the time, it wasn't social taboo to take a lover. After all, Auden had had trysts himself, but he kept those private. One never flaunted a lover, and that extended to blatant public displays of affect which bothered Auden. One time at dinner in Ischia, Auden's friend, Thekla Clark, happened to be openly flirting with her lover, Alberto, at the table.

"You mustn't act like newlyweds," Auden said as he stroked a cat. "Happiness, like grief, should be private."[129]

Instead of keeping things private, Chester had openly defied the social norms by bringing Alessandro to dinner at The Caffè where the rest of the "gang" frequented.

When Auden told Chester that it would be out of the question for him to take Alessandro to Venice, Chester replied smugly, "Well, you're taking me."[130]

The Rake's Progress received rave reviews. Just a few weeks after it opened, other cities such as Hamburg, Düsseldorf, Stuttgart, Rome, and Zurich held their own productions. By the spring of 1953, it *The Rake's Progress* had been performed over two hundred times.[131]

That same year, Auden and Chester moved back to New York and rented the railroad apartment on the second floor on an old tenement building at 77 St. Mark's Place in the East Village just west of 1st Avenue. Built in 1845, it originally had 3 ½ floors, and a fourth floor was added later. Ironically, it was located one block away from The Modern School of New York.

As with all of Auden's apartments, this one soon became notoriously unkempt. Auden's good friend, Hannah Arendt, once described the apartment: "His slum apartment was so cold that the toilet no longer functioned and he had to use the toilet in the liquor store at the corner."[132] Auden once said, "I hate living in squalor—I detest it!—but I can't do the work I want to do and live any other way.'"[133]

In 1956, Auden was hired as Professor of Poetry at Oxford University but was only contracted to give three week-long lectures a year. This gave him free time throughout the year to live as he wanted and enough money to enjoy his apartment in New York during the winter months and spend his summers in Ischia.[134]

Auden got a calico cat in his apartment in St. Mark's Place. He loved all animals especially cats. He had one in England and considered them good luck. He disagreed with the church regarding pets not having souls and was certain that cats possessed souls. I'm not sure about how I feel about cats bringing good luck or whether or not they have souls, but I've always enjoyed our pets. One afternoon, the boys found an abandoned cat and they brought it home. They called her Jingles. Why Jingles? I have no idea, but we all loved her. We also had a Dalmatian dog at one point, too, named Samson. Whether animals have souls or not seems irrelevant to me. Our pets brought warmth and energy to our home, and they gave us so much joy. They were loved.

Ada Calhoun wrote about St. Mark's Place in her book *St. Mark's Is Dead* that the street wasn't for people who had chosen their lives but rather that it was "superglue for fragmented identities…for the wanderer, the undecided, the lonely, and the promiscuous."[135]

That type of hodge podge neighbor sounds exactly where Auden would have felt most at home, padding around the neighborhood in his bedroom slippers. Auden and Chester settled into their domestic life and lived happily in their shabby apartment with their lucky cat for nearly twenty years.

Chapter Twenty

I had also settled into a happy domestic life. I enjoyed raising my boys and working part time in Morty's office making appointments, sorting files, and answering the phone. Morty loved being a pediatrician, and he was a good doctor. He had an incredible amount of patience, not only with the children he treated, but also with the parents.

Of course, we don't use the term "retarded" now. President Obama signed a bill into law on October 5, 2010 known as *Rosa's Law* after a Maryland girl with Down's Syndrome named Rosa Marcellino. The law requires the government to replace the use of the term "mental retardation" with "intellectual disability." Most states and federal agencies had already made that adjustment anyway, but this mandated the change.[136]

Not only did we not think of the R-word as derogatory back then, but most people didn't really understand mental retardation, so Morty got some pretty interesting questions and phone calls. One time, a woman called the office looking for Morty.

"Hello? Is this the number for the retarded doctor?"

Another woman called Morty asking about her daughter's prospects.

"Will she marry?" the woman asked.

The child was so mentally impaired that Morty knew that she would never even be able to tie her shoe laces, but the woman's main concern was that she could one day be married.

During that time in my life, I took a break from writing poetry and seriously took up cooking. I had been collecting cookbooks for a long time, but I never really wanted to write a cook book as was mentioned in the newspaper article. I just wanted to write down my recipes. I had been the president of the PTA at the time, and the newspaper was interviewing me for that. They took pictures of me in

Long Island Daily Press

AUG 31 1953

Cook of the Week   By TESS FITZGERALD

MD's Wife a Kitchen Scientist

Gladys Dubovsky, a doctor's cousin, scarcely ever passes a bookstore without purchasing an addition to her collection of best sellers . . . a library of cookbooks.

And she's rather curl up with a book of recipes than the latest "who-dun-it" or the No. 1 novel of the year.

"The reason I'm boning up is easy to explain," said the attractive Flushing-Hillcrest housewife, "because almost any day now I expect to write my own cookbook."

Gladys, the wife of Dr. Mortimer Dubovsky, believes that cooking is like science. And she makes a good case in drawing up the comparison.

"It's a domestic science," she continued, "that calls for plenty of technical know-how and research. You don't need a degree for it but you do need book-learning."

AND AS evidence, she pointed to her cookbook library, neatly shelved in the Dubovsky kitchen at 153-02 78th avenue. In it are more than 30 editions, some of which date back to the early 1880s.

The latest . . . a handsome volume of 600 pages . . . was presented to her when she retired as president of the Parent-Teacher Association of P. S. 154. Her sons, Steven, 9, and Daniel, 8, are students there.

But the most popular with her family and friends are a few unpretentious books filled with her original recipes.

Gladys has tested, tasted and approved each recipe before entering it in the kitchen archives.

"I guess this system is a carryover from the days I worked as a research librarian," she said.

Her interest in science also plays a part in Mrs. Dubovsky's choice of club work. She's active in the Queens League for Mental Health, the Committee for Mentally Retarded Children and the Flower and Fifth Avenue Hospitals Auxiliary.

WHEN GLADYS entertains friends or her husband's colleagues, a special treat is Swedish meat balls, served as hors d'oeuvres. Here's her recipe:

Mix together a pound of chopped beef, a third of a cup of bread crumbs, one slightly beaten egg, a pinch of pepper, a half of a teaspoon of salt, a few grains of allspice, the grated rind of one lemon and a half of a teaspoon of MSG (monosodium glutamate).

Shape the mixture into small balls about the size of a quarter and brown in butter in a skillet.

BOOK LEARNING: Mrs. Gladys Dubovsky, who believes in cooking by the book, consults a volume from her Flushing-Hillcrest kitchen library.

half of a cup of consomme . . . stirring often.

First season, and then cook the sauce and meat balls in a batch

of a cup of sherry wine and simmer the Swedish delicacy over low flame until it's party time. "Served from a chafing dish on

Move over Julia Child!

the house, and somehow got wind of my cook book collection and the article took off from there. The fact that they called me a "kitchen scientist"—well, that was just silly.

In addition to cooking, I've always had a garden whether it was wherever Morty was stationed or back home in Mohegan. When Steven was a baby, I would put him in his highchair, run out to the garden, and quickly pick carrots or beets and come back and cook it and give it to him. Morty and I also created a beautiful flower bed that ran along the front of the Mohegan house.

We took our first trip to Massachusetts with the boys in the 1950s. Martha's Vineyard was nice, but it was so busy and packed with tourists. We took a day trip to Nantucket and fell in love with the place. It was so quiet and laid back and relaxed that we went back pretty regularly from then on.

We also fell in love with a young painter there named Roy Bailey. He was carefree and seductive in a James Dean kind of way. His gallery was located in a small attic space above Miltimore's Dress Shop on the corner of Orange Street and South Main Street. We bought several of his famous sea-themed paintings of Nantucket Island. After he moved to Vermont and started painting barns, we bought those as well.

We had returned from Europe once to find a note from Roy saying that he was in town and having a one-man show at the Hammer Galleries on East 67th Street. It was the last day of the show, so we ran down to Hammer Galleries to see his collection. I fell in love with a painting of pink flowers in a grey pot, so I called Roy on the phone.

"Roy, I see a painting here, and I want to buy it. If it hasn't already been sold, make me an offer."

"Yes, the pink flowers," Roy said. "I think it was for sale for

This lovely painting still graces my living room wall

$13,000.00. The truth is, I really like that painting, and I think I might keep that one for my own collection."

"If you ever change your mind, give us first refusal."

After I hung up, I said to Morty, "I'll give him a week. He'll want that money."

Sure enough, in less than a week, he called and said we could have it.

Many years later, I travelled back to Nantucket with Steven, Anne, and Dan, and we looked Roy up. He was very sick at the time. He had moved back to Nantucket from Vermont and was living with Nancy Verde Barr who was Julia Childs's secretary. She had written a book about her time with Julia called *Backstage with Julia: My Years with Julia Child.* Roy had also illustrated a cook book. He told us that he and Nancy and Julia were at some big affair together, and he was standing with Julia. A woman came up and said to him, "I love your book!" And Julia Child was standing right beside him, totally ignored.

We chatted a while and looked over the paintings in his house.

"How much are these going for now?" I asked.

"Thirty or forty thousand."

We had purchased one of his very first paintings for $125. Now I think I have fifteen of his paintings.

That was the last time I saw him before he died of prostate cancer in 2002. He was 69.

When Steven turned twelve in 1956, he made an announcement.

"Mom and Dad, I want to have a bar mitzvah," he said.

"But we don't go to Temple," I said. "Look, if you want a party, we'll throw you a party."

"No. All my friends are having a bar mitzvah, so I want one, too."

"Okay, but just remember if you don't do it all the way, the way they do it, it's not going to count."

So, we went to the Reform Synagogue and spoke to the Rabbi.

"Steven," the Rabbi said, "in order to have a bar mitzvah, you have to study for three years. You don't have three years."

The Rabbi shifted in his chair and faced me. "But, if you pay for the three years, and if Steven goes to Sunday school every week, we'll get him through it."

I looked my son in the eye. "Steven, you heard the Rabbi say what you need to do. But if you don't do everything—all the way—it won't count."

Later, Steven was with a few boys on the street corner who were talking about their upcoming bar mitzvahs. Steven mentioned something about his bar mitzvah.

"You don't go to Hebrew school," one of the boys said.

"Yes, I do. I go to Sunday school."

"That doesn't count for Hebrew school." The boys all laughed at Steven.

He came home that afternoon and told me what the boys had said.

"I told you. If you don't do it their way, in their eyes, it won't count."

Undaunted, Steven continued his studies and eventually had his bar mitzvah.

Just before Steven's bar mitzvah, Papa mentioned that Harry had been working with him in his dry cleaning business and that he had a wife, Sadie, and daughter, Helen, who was going to be married. I hadn't spoken to Harry in years, so I decided to invite them to the bar mitzvah. When Harry and I finally saw each other again after so long, there was absolutely no recognition on his part of what he had done to me as a child or that so much time had passed without us communicating. He greeted me as though we had seen each other the previous weekend. Afterwards, Morty and I went to Helen's wedding.

Each spring, Morty and I had our family over for Passover Seder. I remember we made platters piled high with fresh potato pancakes. Even though it was our party, my father loved being the center of attention. It was always all about him. Papa insisted, in addition to my aunt and uncle and cousins, that Harry and Sadie should be invited to come as well. They all gathered around Papa, and he would perform. He always told the Passover story, but he jokingly did it while speaking with a sort of Jewish cockney accent. He addressed Pharaoh as "Fairy," and he'd say, "So, Moses came to Fairy, and he said, 'Hey, Fairy, you gotta let us outta here. If you don't let my people go, God's gonna strike your firs-born dead.'" After the Seder was over and all the food had been eaten, he would sing songs in Yiddish for the assembled company.

After Steven's bar mitzvah, my cousin, George, told me that his son, Burt, also wanted a bar mitzvah.

"Nobody in the family goes to Temple," George said. "We don't do bar mitzvahs. Why do you feel the need to have one all of a sudden?"

"All the boys are having their bar mitzvahs, so I want one, too."

"I'll tell you what. I'll give you a choice. You can have a bar mitzvah, or you can have the money it would cost to have a bar mitzvah."

"How much will a bar mitzvah cost?" Burt asked.

"Twenty-five dollars."

"I'll take the money."

That same year, in the winter of 1956, while Auden and Chester were in New York, Auden forwarded a check for £60,000 to their houseboy, Giocondo, to pay his salary. Unfortunately, Auden forgot to write out the amount of sixty thousand or *sessantamila*. When Giocondo took the check to the bank, an additional zero had been added to the dollar amount. The bank clerk knew the amount was way off. He also knew that Auden didn't have £600,000 in the bank to cover the check, so he refused to cash it.

When word got back to Auden about the check, he suspected that Giocondo tried to pull a fast one and added the zero. Who else would have done that? Nevertheless, when Auden returned the following spring, he found that the whole town, including his friends, had been gossiping about the bad check behind his back. Giocondo had landed a job as a bartender at a local restaurant and gabbed about the check to anyone who would listen. If anyone rejected his tall tale, Giocondo refused to let them enter the restaurant. Regardless of the truth, the damage was done. The town believed that Giocondo had been cheated by Auden.[137]

In 1957, Auden spent the year alone in Ischia. Chester decided to stay behind in New York. In February 1957, Auden spent his 50th birthday with Thekla Clark. She brought two small legs of lamb back to Ischia with her from Florence to cook for his birthday party. Auden was grateful for all the well-wishes from friends at the party and from the many telegrams he received from all over the world, but overall, Auden was lonely and melancholy. He passed much of the time by himself and took long walks. On one of these walks with Thekla Clark, Auden contemplated the theory of male menopause.

"What is that like for a woman?" he asked. "What are hot flashes like?"

"I have no idea. I'm only thirty."

"You women are so fortunate. You know why you're here. I'm adrift. I'm a clown."

"A sacred one," Thekla joked.

"No, but a transatlantic one. The way you Americans mark the passage of time, you do it with hope."

They walked on quietly along the shore. Around a bend, they noticed a bum leaning against a rock, masturbating while gazing out at the sea. If Auden wasn't in a funk before that display, that was sure to have put him over the edge. He and Thekla decided to head back to the village and have a stiff drink.[138]

On May 3rd, Auden's father, George Augustus Auden, died at the age of eighty-five. Luckily, he was able to be with his father at the end. That June, Auden won a lifetime achievement award from the *Feltrinelli Prize* also known as the *Italian Lincei Literary Prize.* The award was 20,000,000 lire or about $32,000.00—the largest amount of money that Auden had ever been paid.[139] After he returned to Ischia after his father's funeral, he thought about buying the house he had been renting. When the landlord found out about Auden's prize money, he jacked up the asking price.

Ischia had always been enchanting, but all that glitters is not gold. Years earlier, one of Auden's cats, his favorite blue-eyed white beauty named Lucina, was poisoned. He buried her under an orange tree and wrote a sweet poem, *In Memoriam, L.K.A. 1950-1952,* in her honor.

> At peace under this mandarin, sleep, Lucina,
> Blue-eyed Queen of white cats
> For you the Ischian wave
> Shall weep
> When we who now miss you
> Are American dust
> And steep Epomeo in peace and war
> Augustly a grave-watch keep.[140]

The death of Lucina, his greedy landlord, and the Giocondo nastiness soured him on Ischia. Maybe it was because of his father's death, but Auden was feeling homesick for the north. He and Chester had been talking about where they wanted to put down roots. They both agreed that they wanted to live in a place where German was spoken, but not Germany. The place had to have decent wine to drink and should have access to the excellent opera.[141]

It was time for Auden to make his next big move.

Chapter Twenty-One

That is my home of love: if I have ranged,
Like him that travels, I return again
— William Shakespeare, *Sonnet 109*

I n 1925, Auden travelled to Vienna with his father and was enchanted with the place, so it's no surprise that he chose Austria to find his home. In the spring of 1958, he and Chester found a converted farmhouse on three acres of green lawn nestled beside the Vienna Woods in the village of Kirchstetten just twenty-nine miles west of Vienna. The mud-spattered house had small cozy rooms with whitewashed walls and peasant-type furniture. Chester persuaded Auden to renovate the kitchen. A chicken run led to Auden's study.[142] His studio, the attic, had a desk beneath a window that looked out over a duck pond and the surrounding countryside.[143] Auden was said to have shed tears of joy at owning a home for the very first time.[144] Although he spoke of the property as "my land," he always referred to the house with Chester in mind as "our house."[145]

Chester took to the place like a fish to water planting a vegetable garden and growing morning glories. It was a flower they both adored, and they strung them up along the porch railings as a tribute to Ischia.[146] Auden and Chester would begin their days on the porch among their morning glories. Chester with a huge mug of iced coffee and his work, and Auden no doubt with tea and a cigarette, counting the flowers as they opened their eager faces to the morning sun. One spring in New York, Auden was fit to be tied after he found that there were no morning glory seeds to be had anywhere in the city to take back with him to Kirchstetten.

Apparently, the teenagers at that time were eating them to get high. Luckily, Thekla Clark was able to mail him some from Italy. "God bless Italia," he wrote her after the package arrived.[147]

The villagers were thrilled to have a famous poet as their neighbor, and Auden became active in the community attending school meetings, volunteering, debating what to do about the roads, and giving speeches. He was finally, truly content.

Auden in Kirchstetten.
Photo by Harry Redl ©The LIFE Picture Collection
Getty Images

Auden and Chester happily spent their summers in their cozy country farm house in Kirchstetten working on several librettos together. They travelled back and forth to New York to their Greenwich Village apartment in the winters. Auden loved that six months out of the year he could get Polish and Jewish food anytime he wanted in Manhattan and hail a cab 24/7. Chester no longer enjoyed the cold weather, so in 1963, he decided to spend the rest of his winters in Athens, Greece instead of New York.

While Auden loved Austria, I hated it. Morty and I went on a trip to Vienna with the Mental Retardation Institute. While he was at the conference, I decided to see the sights of Vienna, specifically Sigmund Freud's house. Trouble was, I couldn't find a single taxi driver who knew the address.

Later that night, our delegation of about 150 people were all invited to a special reception by the Mayor of Vienna who happened to be Jewish. When I happened to mention that the cab drivers couldn't find Sigmund Freud's house, he shook his head.

"They know exactly where his house is, but they won't tell you."

"Why not?"

"Because, I'm ashamed to say, anti-Semitism is alive and well in Vienna. I'll make sure you see his house."

The following morning, the Mayor put my friend Harold and me in a cab and told the driver exactly where to go.

Afterwards, we took a bus tour through Vienna. The tour guide was a stocky woman who I swear could have walked right off the set of the Alfred Hitchcock movie *The Lady Vanishes* with her hat and tweeds and Stalwart boots. She stood at the front of the bus facing us and waved her hand at either side of the bus as if she were Vanna White.

"Over here," she said, "we had a beautiful subway, but the Americans bombed it." She motioned toward the other side of the bus.

"And over here, we had a beautiful church, but the English bombed it. And over here, we had a beautiful factory, but that was bombed by the Americans, too."

"Yes," I said, "and all the while the Viennese were burning up people. Harold, we're getting off this bus"

We made them stop the bus, and we got off.

Later that week, another friend of mine, Ines Riggio, and I went to the famous Hotel Sacher to buy their famous Austrian Sacher-Torte, which is an elegant, chocolate sponge cake with apricot jam and dark chocolate icing. You can't go to Austria and not try a Sacher-Torte!

Ines and I were buying Sacher-Torte to be sent back to the United States. We had theater tickets for later that evening, so I leaned forward to catch the eye of the woman packing up our cakes.

"We have tickets to the opera tonight," I said. "Do people dress for the opera?" What I wanted to know was would the women be wearing long gowns only or would some women wear shorter cocktail dresses.

"Well, they most certainly do dress, except those dirty American hippies who come here and don't know how to dress for our opera."

"Do you really expect that the young people travelling with a backpack would pack a tuxedo to go to the Viennese opera?"

She left the cake boxes on the counter and came and stood before me. "I most certainly do, and if not, they have no right to come!"

"I think Vienna should put a sign around her borders saying 'Visitors Unwelcome.' As for me, I've already seen that sign on the faces of the Viennese people I've met here. So, you can keep your Sacher-Torte."

I stormed out of the shop onto the sidewalk. Ines ran to catch up with me.

"I can't believe you said that," she said, laughing.

"Believe it."

It was on that same trip that we were going from Vienna to Budapest on one of the three buses we had rented. There were three nuns on our bus. When we got to the border, our tour guide stood and faced us.

"We're stopping for a minute, but I don't want any of you to get off the bus. This area is mine territory. The land along the border still contains buried land mines.

One of the nuns shook her head. "If I lived this close to Vienna, I'd mine my borders, too."

I really hated Vienna. Nobody got into as much trouble as I did. I know other people who have been to Vienna since, and they don't report such crap. Maybe it's because I call people out on their bologna. I don't mince words, and I don't suffer fools lightly. Never have. Never will.

Chapter Twenty-Two

I n 1960, I read an article in the *New York Times* about a book written by a man named Irv Werstein called *The blizzard of '88*. I knew Irv Werstein in my last year in high school. He was one of the friends who went with me to that first party at Morty's house. I looked him up in the telephone book. It said that he was living on East 20th Street in Manhattan, so I dialed his number.

"Irv Werstein," I said.

"Yes. Who is this?"

"This is Gladys Levy, Gladys Dubovsky, now. I'm not sure if you remember me—"

"Remember you? Gladys of course, I remember you. You're the reason I became a writer!"

Just before my senior year in high school, we moved from the Colony to Richmond Hill in Queens, which was a very straight-laced community. I was different from all the other students there. I read a lot of books and was interested in all kinds of literary things. Apparently, I had inspired Irv. He hadn't been in contact with anyone like me before I had moved there. What I find interesting is that we never once talked about books or writing all the time we were friends, nevertheless, my passion had influenced him without me even knowing it. Irv went on to write about forty books. I recently picked up *The blizzard of '88* from my bookshelf and started to reread it. He was a really good writer. Irv died on Wednesday, April 7, 1971 of a heart attack. He was only 57 years old.

Morty and I often drove up to the Colony on the weekends to relax. The Colony had always been home for me. It's very different now. Over the years, as people died out and others outside the community bought up the houses, our tight community began to fall apart. They sold the school building and the tennis courts to a church. I don't know anyone who lives there anymore. For a time, my whole family lived there. I couldn't walk down the road without hitting a cousin. Back then, it was a beautiful place to live. We had community property, tennis courts, and of course, the school. There was a pavilion where they gave concerts and performances. There was the crystal-clear lake with the beach front property that belonged to the Colony.

One of those weekends, I met up with my friend, Lydia, who had married our mutual friend from the Colony, Normie Miller. One afternoon, Lydia and I decided to leave our husbands and lay out in the sun on the beach along the lake.

"I had a long talk with Yonk Kling the other day," Lydia said straightening her towel in the sand and lay down.

I propped myself up onto an elbow. "I remember Yonk. He introduced me to Reggie Wilson."

"We talked about him."

"How is Reggie?"

Lydia sat up. "Reggie is dead."

I sat up. "I'm sorry to hear that. Was it cancer?"

"No, it wasn't cancer. Reggie was head over heels in love with you, you know. By the end of the summer you two spent together, he saw that you and Morty were getting serious, and that broke his heart."

"He never told me any of this."

Lydia shrugged. "He told Yonk that all he wanted was for you to be happy. That's why he stopped coming around. He didn't want to get in the way of your happiness. After that, he said he needed to do something to occupy his mind, so he traveled to Europe and eventually to Spain where he fought with the Republicans in their Civil War. He was killed in battle."

"I had no idea that Reggie was in love with me. I was the reason he needed to get away. I was the reason he fought in Spain and died."

Things happen for a reason. When Ben stopped writing to me after that wonderful summer we shared, he made it clear to me that he was no longer interested in me, so I had to move on. I really liked Reggie, but he never told me how he felt about me and backed off his courtship. There was a reason these relationships fizzled. Even if things had been different and Ben or Reggie had continued to court me, I still would have married Morty, because we were meant to be together. Be that as it may, I wish I had known that Reggie loved me. I don't know if I could have done or said anything to keep him from going away and joining the war in Spain, but knowing what I know now, I would have tried my hardest to make him stay.

The character, Rick, in my favorite movie *Casablanca*, Auden, and Reggie—all involved in the Spanish Civil War. Six degrees of separation. It's incredible how we influence each other—many times without even knowing it. Because of me, Irv Werstein became a writer and wrote 40 books. And, directly or indirectly, because of me, Reggie went to war and died. Auden taught me, encouraged me, and gave me confidence. Because of him, I knew I mattered.

All this makes me think of the movie *It's a Wonderful Life*. You have no idea just how much your life affects other people's lives. And you may never be aware that you're influencing others with the choices that you make. But you influence them all the same.

The 1960s saw a lot of changes for me and Morty. Morty's father, Ben, contracted an infection in his bladder. On Wednesday, September 11, 1963, he died of septicemia caused by the infection.

The following October, Papa called me on the phone.

"Your mother is lying on the bathroom floor, and she won't wake up."

My parents were living in an apartment in Woodside, Queens about a twenty-minute drive from our house in Flushing. Morty called my cousin and her husband who lived a block away from us to go over to my parent's apartment with us. Although Morty was a doctor, my cousin's husband, Seymour Carlin, was also a doctor. I think Morty wanted to get a second opinion in case one was needed. As it turned out, that wasn't necessary. As soon as they saw Mama, it was clear that she was dead. The coroner said that she had died of a heart attack.

My mother and Steven had such a close relationship, and I'm certain their bond was formed in part because of the circumstances of his birth. My mother had come out to Colorado for the birth, but all the while I was sick, she stayed with me in the hospital. It was touch and go for a while, and I nearly died. She later told me that while I slept, she would often walk down the hall and stand in front of the nursery window and watch Steven sleep in his crib. She would cry whenever she thought about what would happen to that poor baby if he lost his mother. When I finally came out of the hospital with Steven, who had colic, and screamed constantly, my mother was the one who carried him and held him and cooed to him all the time. A strong bond developed between them, and it was clear that they had a very special relationship. She was there for him when nobody else was.

Because they had always been very close, Mama's death was hard on Steven. After he graduated from high school, he decided to go to college at Harpur College in Binghamton for his bachelor's degree. I found out later that he would often come home to Queens for the weekend that first year in college and stay with Mama and go back on Sunday afternoon. He never told me he was even in town. She never told me either.

Whereas Morty was expected to go into medicine, Steven decided that on his own. I should say that we never pushed him, but that my mother wanted him to be a doctor. Many years after Mama's death and after he graduated from NYU School of Medicine, he wrote a book and dedicated it to her saying, "To Nan, who always wanted me to be a doctor."

Many years later when my first granddaughter was born, Steven and his wife Anne called me to ask about my mother.

"What was your mother's name?" Anne asked. "Steven and I want to name our daughter after her."

"Her name is Sonia," I said, "but the kids all call her Nan."

They named their daughter Amelia Nan Dubovsky.

A year later, Morty's mother, Lena, died. She had been in a nursing home for some time. I'm not sure exactly when or how she died. I think I have no recollection of her death at all because I really didn't care.

A few years later, Papa contracted bladder cancer and died. There is no history of cancer in my family, but Papa used to clean all the machines by himself in his dry cleaner. PERC, or the chemical perchloroethylene or tetrachloroethylene is the chemical used in dry cleaners. In 2008, the EPA suggested the PERC be classified as a "likely human carcinogen."[148] Without knowing how dangerous this chemical was, Papa was exposed to it every day. It's found in the air, in the water, and in the surrounding soil. He was in the hospital about two weeks before he succumbed. I wasn't there when he died. He was about 90.

In the span of those few short years, Morty and I lost both our parents. We weren't the only ones to feel the pain of loss. In the midst of it all, the world watched as a bright light was suddenly snuffed out in Dallas, Texas. On November 22, 1963, just past his first thousand days in office, President Kennedy was shot dead smiling at the cheering crowds while riding in the presidential motorcade through Dealey Plaza.

Like millions of people around the world, Auden was shocked and deeply saddened by the news. He had traveled to Washington, D.C. in January 1961 and stood with thousands of parade goers in the rain and watched the newly inaugurated John F. Kennedy pass by. He was convinced that the young, vibrant president waving to the crowds would bring renewed hope and prosperity to the country.[149]

Two months after JFK's death, Auden learned that Stravinsky had planned to compose an elegy to Kennedy. Auden suggested that he write the words to that elegy. The following month, Auden sent Stravinsky his *Elegy for J.F.K.*

> When a just man dies,
> Lamentation and praise,
> Sorrow and joy, are one.
>
> Why then, why there,
> Why thus, we cry, did he die?
> The heavens are silent.
>
> What he was, he was:
> What he is fated to become
> Depends on us

Remembering his death,
How we choose to live
Will decide its meaning.

When a just man dies,
Lamentation and praise,
Sorrow and joy, are one.[150]

It's first performance, using a baritone and three clarinets, was given in Los Angeles on April 6, 1964.[151]

Like everyone else in the world, I remember exactly where I was when I found out that President Kennedy had been killed. Morty was seeing patients that morning, and I was in his office working. Someone came in the office and said that the president had been killed. I ran in and told Morty. Understandably, everybody was so upset.

I was convinced that LBJ shot him. I hated that guy at the time. My hatred of him had to do with the Vietnam war, you see. He was my enemy. On December 1, 1969, the Selective Service System of the United States conducted two lotteries to determine the order of call to military service in the Vietnam War for men born from 1944 to1950.[152] That meant that both of my sons were eligible for the draft. I was vehemently against the war, and there was no way I was going to let my sons go fight in Vietnam. No way, no how. That was all I thought about in terms of LBJ in his early years.

After JFK was shot, LBJ had the enormous pressure of having to step into those shoes. JFK was a beloved and revered president. He was young and handsome and popular. LBJ was none of those things. He was filled with doubt and fear. I think one's true nature comes out when they are under the most stress, and LBJ rose up and overcame his fears.

Nothing in life is black and white, and with LBJ, it was like a tale of two presidents. Without the Vietnam War, he would have been one of the greatest presidents of all time next to FDR. He never let the grass grow under his feet, and he expected the same from everyone in office. He insisted that members of Congress return a phone call or answer a request that same day even if it meant finding that person and chasing them down on the street or in a bar or in a bathroom. Can you imagine that happening with today's Congress? His personal motto was, "Do it now. Not next week. Not tomorrow. Not later today. Now." LBJ submitted, and Congress then enacted, more than one hundred major proposals in each of the 89th and 90th Congresses. Just look at what he was able to accomplish: the *Civil Rights Act*, the *Voting Rights Act*, *Head Start*, the *Elementary and Secondary Education Act*, the *Fair Housing Act*, *Medicare*, *Medicaid*, the *Clean Air Act*, the *Clean Water Act*, the *National Endowment for the Arts*—just to name a few—all in order to make the world a fair and better place for everyone.[153]

I don't want to paint the picture that LBJ was some sort of saint. On the contrary, he was not a nice man to deal with. He was a bully, and he cheated on his wife. But with regards to political policy, he accomplished a great deal of good things for so many people.

When we look back on presidents like FDR and LBJ, we see what a highly-qualified leader is able to accomplish. Compare that to President Trump who is not only someone who doesn't understand government, but he doesn't have the desire and humility to learn anything. Will we ever see another man or woman to lead our country like FDR or LBJ? I have my doubts, but I sure hope so.

Chapter Twenty-Three

Evil is unspectacular and always human,
And shares our bed and eats at our own table.
— W. H. Auden, *Herman Melville*

D ag Hammarskjöld was a Swedish diplomat, economist, and author who served as the second Secretary-General of the United Nations, from April 1953 until his death in a plane crash in northern Rhodesia (now Zambia) on September 18, 1961. He had been on a peace-keeping mission to help end a war in Congo, a former Belgian colony rich in mining. Powerful people would have killed for the rights to those vital minerals. He had been on his way to oversee cease-fire negotiations. Former President Harry Truman was convinced that Hammarskjöld was murdered, and that the plane crash was brought down on purpose. Rumors swirled around Hammarskjöld's final hours with some reports saying there were intercepted radio transmissions that tracked the plane as it made its final descent, and that airplanes had been parked along the darkened runway. The plane went down just minutes from landing. These same reports claim that his plane had been riddled with bullets. Although official findings hint at pilot error, enough questions remain—

enough to warrant the ongoing inquiries into the crash and purport-
ed radio transmissions.

The crash set off a chain of events throughout the African conti-
nent causing wars from Mozambique and Zimbabwe to Angola and
Namibia between those who wanted to keep a tight rein on their
colonialism and those who fought for independence—all that culmi-
nating later with the end of apartheid in South Africa.[154]

Interestingly, I read about Auden's connection to Dag Hammarskjöld years later while sitting in my apartment in Midtown located
along Dag Hammarskjöld Plaza. In 1964, Auden wrote a forward for
Hammarskjöld's posthumous book, *Vägmärken* or *Markings*, hint-
ing that Hammarskjöld had been a homosexual, but never acted on
his desires.

Auden was Dag Hammarskjöld's candidate for the Nobel Prize
and was thought to be a shoe in to win until the unhappy Swedish
Academy read the forward that he wrote. They thought it was simply
too scandalous to support, so they asked him to remove any immod-
est references. Normally, Auden would have no problem rewriting
his work for publishers or editors unless he felt that the rewrite would
in any way be dishonest. In this case, Auden refused to rewrite the
forward and commented to a friend at dinner that night, "There goes
the Nobel Prize."[155]

We humans have such capacity for kindness and compassion,
and yet, we are cursed with the need to plot against one another,
and for what? From ancient times, we have cooked up ways to kill
each other, berate each other, lord our power over each other. It's our
human nature I suppose. Our Good versus Evil. Our Yin and Yang.

As Auden sat in his attic in Kirchstetten and looked out onto the
green countryside, he thought about how wonderful life was and also
how terrible we humans can make it if we allow the evil that resides
inside all of us to rear its ugly head. We should never ever be lulled

into complacency and think that the malevolence of the past will stay in the past. We humans have a sad knack of repeating history. Here is an excerpt from his poem *The Cave of Making*:

More than ever
life-out-there is goodly, miraculous, loveable,
    but we shan't, not since Stalin and Hitler,
trust ourselves ever again: we know that, subjectively,
    all is possible. (lines 45-49)[156]

I overheard or read someone say that the political atmosphere today feels like the 1900s. I thought about how WWI started. On June 28, 1914, Archduke Franz Ferdinand, who was heir to the Austro-Hungarian Empire, and his wife, Sophie, rode through the streets of Sarajevo in an open car. Austria-Hungary had just annexed the Balkans and the Serbians were furious. As they drove through the crowds in their open car, someone threw a bomb at them, but it bounced off the car and injured several people. Later, the Archduke and his wife went to visit the injured and their driver took a wrong turn and drove right past another Serbian nationalist who took out his gun and shot them, killing them both.[157]

The assassination started a chain of events that culminated in war. Many countries blamed the Serbian government for the attack, but Russia (with allies France and Britain) backed Serbia. Austria-Hungary sought support from the Germans. On July 28, Austria-Hungary declared war on Serbia. Russia, Belgium, France, Great Britain and Serbia sided against Austria-Hungary and Germany. World War I had begun.[158]

Peace is precious and tenuous. It doesn't take much to upset the balance. WWII began with Germany's unprovoked attack on Poland on September 1, 1939. As I read the news about nuclear tensions rising between the United States and North Korea, I can't help but think back on the Cuban Missile Crisis in the 1960s. Thank goodness, all parties back then stood down. All it takes is one false move, one misunderstanding, one angry or insulting Tweet, and our delicate peace-balance can be hopelessly tipped.

Chapter Twenty-Four

I think I knew my son Dan was gay before he did. In fact, two of our very dear friends, Dr. Harold Michal-Smith and Dr. Murray Morganstern, were gay. They were both psychologists who worked in the Mental Retardation Institute with Morty. We had been invited to a party at Harold's house, and at that time he was still married to a nice woman named Sylvia. It wasn't long after that party that Harold and Murray fell in love. Even though Harold and Sylvia divorced, they remained good friends.

By the time Dan had reached his late teens or early twenties, he still hadn't come out, so I asked Harold for his advice.

"I'm certain Dan is gay," I said, "but I don't know what to say to him."

"Just mention it to him."

I thought about it but decided not to say anything. After all, it wasn't my news to tell. I just had to wait for him to bring it up in his own time, if he wanted. As it turned out, he never really came out officially to us. He never sat us down and made any sort of announcement. It was one of those things that just naturally fell into place without any bells or whistles. Dan knew that Morty and I were fine with homosexuality, because our friends were gay, so he knew that there would never be an issue. It was a perfectly natural progression of growth, love, and unspoken understanding.

By the late 1960s, Auden no longer felt the need to hide his homosexuality. At the universities where he would give poetry readings, he sometimes arranged to speak at the students's homosexual societies on campus.[159] He had no desire to join any demonstration groups or rallies, but he felt that he had come to a point in his life and his professional career that he could afford to drop a veil or two without fear of retribution.

In the fall of 1967, Auden's beloved housekeeper, Emma Eiermann or Frau Emma, suddenly died of a heart attack. She and her brother had been Sudeten German refugees from Czechoslovakia and had cared for the house and garden for years. She was strong-willed, grumpy, suspicious of strangers, and completely devoted to Auden. He was terribly sad at her death and even wrote a poem about her saying, "a housekeeper is harder to replace than a lover."[160]

We hired a few maids over the years and grew quite attached to them as well. One of our maids, Barbara, was from Sweden. She was a pretty blonde girl about 18 years old. She worked a few days a week for us and the other days at a nearby dry cleaning store.

One day, her uncle told us that Barbara was very ill in the hospital. Morty and I rushed over to see her, but by the time we got there, she was barely conscious.

"What happened," I asked.

"Barbara was raped, we think by her boss, and she found out she was pregnant," her uncle said.

"Oh my God." I had to sit down in a nearby chair.

"She found someone to give her an abortion," her uncle continued, "but there were complications."

This all happened before Roe v Wade, so abortions were still illegal. I thought of our poor, sweet Barbara having to go to one of those horrid back alley places—someone's kitchen table I can only imagine, and an icy chill rushed through me.

The nurse came in to take her temperature. She looked at the thermometer and shook her head.

"106."

Just then, Barbara's eyes fluttered open. I reached for her hand.

"Barbara," I said, "why didn't you call us? You know we love you. We would have helped you."

"I was too ashamed." She closed her eyes and fell back asleep.

The next day, Barbara slipped into a coma, and she died a few days later. Her death was so tragic and needless. Had we known, we could have helped her. Had this horrible incident happened a few years later, Roe v Wade would have allowed her to safely have an abortion. She would have lived.

During the end of the 1960s, Auden experienced a string of bad luck. A few months after Frau Emma died, Auden crashed his car into a telegraph pole. He was on his way home to Kirchstetten when he tried to catch the eggs he bought from rolling off the passenger seat. He broke his right shoulder which took several painful weeks to heal. Then, Chester's boyfriend, Yannis Boras, was killed while driving Auden's car from Greece to Kirchstetten. Although Chester soon found another lover, he mourned Yannis's death and began to drink even more heavily by starting his day with ouzo at breakfast.[161]

Despite the setbacks, Auden was an optimist. While attending *Poetry International* in London that summer, Auden reflected on his life in an interview by the *Sun* on July 12, 1969 by saying, "I don't want to lose any of my past. No. But I've had an exceptionally lucky life. I got a decent education. I was loved by my parents. I was sometimes unhappy, but I was never bored. I've been allowed to do what

I wanted to do. Why the hell should I complain?"[162]

Back in New York a few years later, Auden's dear friend, Elizabeth Mayer suffered a stroke and was sent to live in a nursing home. He visited her often, taking the subway and bus to get to the far reaches of the Bronx. His visits cheered her up and pleased her family, but he hated being in that place. He even wrote a poem called *Old People's Home* about the "inmates" there.[163] Here's an excerpt.

> As I ride the subway
>   to spend half-an-hour with one, I revisage
> who she was in the pomp and sumpture of her hey-day,
>   when week-end visits were a presumptive joy,
> not a good work. Am I cold to wish for a speedy
>   painless dormition, pray, as I know she prays,
> that God or Nature will abrupt her earthly function?
> (lines 25-31)[164]

It was about this time that Auden found living in New York challenging. His once bohemian St. Mark's Place neighborhood had become filthy and crime ridden. Garbage piled on streets. His apartment wasn't much better. Auden complained that it was falling down around his ears. In addition to the general dark and clutter, he wrote that, "My kitchen roof leaks. A blind is broken. Cockroaches abound. O New York!"[165]

Friends noted that Auden's general mental and physical health were failing as well. They thought that spending so much time writing in isolation may have had something to do with it. He wore the same clothes for months at a time. One friend tried to talk him into buying two suits so that when one was at the cleaners he could wear the other, but he refused. He continued to drink heavily and chain smoked Lucky Strikes. One friend pointed out that he must smoke fifteen thousand cigarettes a year, and he retorted, "Ah, but I don't inhale!"

His friends noticed that his breathing had become labored and that his lips sometimes appeared blue. His long-time doctor in New York had died of pancreatic cancer, and his doctor in Kirchstetten retired shortly after that. For some reason, he was reluctant to find another doctor.[166] He was aware of his own decline, and he simply soldiered on. Even as his health deteriorated, Auden managed to keep up his busy travel schedule frequently flying from New York to Austria to London.

Chapter Twenty-Five

Morty and I also kept a busy travelling schedule. He was often asked to speak at conferences, schools, or symposiums throughout the world that focused on mental retardation, and I went with him. I remember one time, Morty, our friend, Ines Riggio, and I were in Madrid attending one of Morty's conferences. On one of the free days, we decided to hire a car and driver to take us to Toledo. It was only about an hour and a half away, but as soon as we set off, I realized I had to go to the bathroom.

"Can you ask the driver to stop somewhere," I whispered to Morty who was sitting in the front seat next to the driver.

He rolled his eyes. "You always do this."

"Can I help it if I have a bladder the size of a teaspoon?"

So, Morty tried to communicate what I needed in Spanish as best he could. The driver finally pulled up in front of a convent.

"I can't go in with you," the driver said in broken English, "but you ladies can go in, and the nuns will take care of you."

Ines and I climbed out of the backseat and stretched our legs. A pair of storks had built a nest on the convent rook. We walked over to the door and knocked. A small, stocky nurse-looking nun came and opened the door.

"May we please use your bathroom?" I asked.

"Absolutely," she said.

I gave Morty and the driver a thumbs up and followed the nun inside. She led us up a long flight of stairs to a room that had a tub, sink, and toilet. She flashed her palm for us to wait. She disappeared and came back with a pail of water and began filling the tub. We had asked for the bathroom, and she thought we wanted to take a bath. Can you imagine her thinking we stopped along the way just to take a bath?

"No, no! That." I pointed to the toilet.

The three of us were hysterical.

"Well, you asked for the bathroom," Ines said.

I tell you, we were laughing so hard I barely made it to the toilet. After we did our business, the three of us went tumbling down the stairs, still in stitches.

In November of 1971, Morty and I were asked to teach at a school for people with mental retardation in Uruguay. When we arrived in Montevideo, we were told to immediately sign in with the American Embassy.

"I don't know what you're doing here," the man at the embassy said. "The elections are to be held at the end of the month. This is the worst time to be here. Do yourselves a favor, don't go to the same place two days in a row, and don't go the same route."

"We'll be working a block away from the hotel," I said. "How many different ways can we take to get there?"

"Truthfully, I'm required to tell you all this, but honestly, I wouldn't worry too much," the man said. "You're not that kidnappable. The Tupamaros are the left-wing group here who are responsible for most of the kidnapping, but they don't kill anybody. Frankly, I keep hoping to be kidnapped, because then I'd get an instant promotion!"

Just as the man at the embassy said, the elections were held at the end of the month. Uruguay had a remarkable election procedure. At the time, there were several parties in the hunt, but three stood out from the rest: National Party, Frente Amplio or the Broad Front, and the Colorado Party. Each party was entitled to one day to demonstrate without interruption. They could do anything they wanted—speak on TV and radio, advertise in newspapers, hold rallies and parades. It was their day to campaign without interference from the opposition. There seemed to be about 100,000 people rooting for the Colorados on their day. There were almost 3 million people in Uruguay with about 1 million living in Montevideo. The Frente Amplio, which was their left-wing coalition party, had about 500,000 people rooting for them, but they lost the election.

Morty and I left soon after the election. We met a couple in the airport who overheard us speaking English. They assumed because we were American that we had been sent to Uruguay by the CIA. They were there as members of the American Institute for Free Labor Development (AIFLD) which was an organization whose sole purpose was to undermine progressive foreign unions by siding with repressive governments. It received its funding from the United States government and was notoriously linked to the CIA.[167]

"Well, we did great," the woman said to me.

"Excuse me?" I asked.

"The election. We got the Colorados in. My husband is on his way to Chile for their election."

It made the hair stand up on the back of my neck. I was so frightened. We were there that whole month and saw and heard the attitude of the people and how the large majority of the people were for the Frente Amplio. The crowds far outnumbered those of the Colorados by about five to one, and yet, our government was able to somehow tip that election in our favor—despite what the majority of the people wanted. It was proof that we had meddled in their election, and that this couple was on their way to tip another election our way. It made me sick.

We saw in the news that seventeen of our intelligence agencies had conclusive evidence that Russia meddled in our 2016 election. It's terrible, but it's clear that our government has done the very same thing in other countries' elections. That does not in any way excuse what the Russians did. It was wrong, but it was just as wrong when we did it.

About that time, Morty was diagnosed with prostate cancer. We discussed the pros and cons of the surgery.

"There's a lot to think about," Morty said. "We have to consider the side effects."

"If you're referring to the possibility of you becoming impotent, well you can get that worry right out of your head. I don't care about the sex. I want you to be alive."

After more back and forth debating and my persistence, he finally agreed to have the surgery. And afterwards, he was fine. It didn't slow him down at all. Most important, he was cancer free!

While Morty's health improved, Auden's declined even further. When Auden returned to New York in 1971, his friend, V. S. Yanovsky, immediately noticed that he was wasting away. In those later years, Auden wrote three major works: *City without Walls and Many Other Poems (1969), Epistle to a Godson and Other Poems (1972),* and the posthumously published *Thank You, Fog: Last Poems (1974).* Many have remarked that Auden's poetry transformed from "an enfant terrible" in his early years to that of a wise reflective grandfather figure—a figure that very much suited him.[168]

Auden embraced the natural cycles of life and seemed resigned to the fact that his health was rapidly declining. His editor, Edward

Mendelson, noted that while in the 1920s Auden wrote of social decays, by the 1970s, he had begun to write of his own internal shutting down. It was clear that he knew he didn't have much time. The last lines of a poem that Auden wrote a year to the day before his death do not appear in any of his published writings. Mendelson wrote them down in the introductory notes in Auden's final volume of poetry *Thank You, Fog*:

> He still loves life
> But OOOO how he wishes
> The good Lord would take him.[169]

It was only in Kirchstetten with Chester where Auden felt most at home and sheltered. When Chester was wintering in Greece, or whenever Auden flew back to England to teach at Oxford or back to New York to the apartment at St. Mark's Place, Auden was despondent. He was lonely. Alcohol was altering him negatively and his health suffered. In addition to the massive amount of alcohol and cigarettes taking their toll, he had been diagnosed with a "defective ticker."

"At my age," Auden said, "it's not good to be alone. Supposing I had a coronary. It might be days before I was found."[170]

In December 1971, he met Stravinsky, his wife, Vera, and Robert Craft for dinner.

"I've just done Igor's obituary for *The Observer*," Auden announced. It was a strange thing to say, but he explained that this was his way of showing his love and admiration. At about 9:00 p.m., Auden bid his guests goodnight and excused himself from dinner as it was getting to be his bedtime. He had no idea at the time that it would be the last time he spoke to Stravinsky who died four months later.[171]

Despite his own failing health, he was more popular than ever. He frequently received letters and phone calls from strangers and celebrities who told him just how much they loved his poetry. Of course, with the sweet comes the sour. The hate mail rolled in as well. One time, he picked up the phone in New York, and the voice said, "We are going to castrate you and then kill you." Before he hung up, in typical Auden fashion, he calmly quipped, "I think you have the wrong number."[172]

On his sixty-fifth birthday, his last in New York, Random House threw him and a group of his friends a combination birthday/going away party in a private room at the Coffee House on West Forty-Fifth Street. Champagne flowed. Toasts were given, and eulogies read. At one point, V. S. Yanovsky threw his champagne glass against the wall "Breaking it skillfully with a good musical tone." Someone else raised a glass to toast Auden.

"I don't know what genius is—"

"Well, who does?" replied Auden.[173]

The truth was, Auden was happy to be leaving New York, not because he disliked the city or the United States. On the contrary, it was a combination of Oxford offering him a small cottage where he could winter for next to nothing, and the fact that New York was becoming too dangerous. He feared he might be mugged. In his tiny apartment in New York, he felt isolated, whereas in Oxford, even if he was lonely, he was never alone.[174]

Chapter Twenty-Six

Every disease is a musical problem;
every cure is a musical solution.

— Novalis

Another one of the countless people who were profoundly influenced by Auden was Dr. Oliver Sacks. Dr. Sacks was a British neurologist, naturalist, historian of science, and an author. He often said that while growing up in England, Auden's poetry was among his formative books.[175]

He had been introduced to Auden in the late 1960s at a party by a mutual friend, but he was too shy to speak to him. Rather, Dr. Sacks stood off to the side of the room and gazed at Auden's "Jurassic face" with awe.

Auden was shy as well, but the two started a friendship that would last until Auden's death. They corresponded in letters, and for the first three years, referred to each other as Dr. Sacks and Mr. Auden. It wasn't until 1971 when Auden sent a typed script of a poem to him, then hand wrote a short note at the bottom which started, "Dear Oliver, if I may…"

They often met at his St. Mark's Place apartment for tea, which was held at 4:00 p.m. sharp, followed by drinking at 5:00 p.m. sharp. They talked about all sorts of things, Auden was particularly interested in Dr. Sack's study of encephalitis lethargica, the sleepy sickness. Auden's father had been an expert in the disease. He wanted to see the patients whom his father studied, so Dr. Sacks brought him to Beth Abraham Hospital where those patients were being cared for. Auden was fascinated by how the speechless could sing and the motionless could dance.[176]

Up until that point, Dr. Sacks hadn't published anything. He showed Auden the book he was writing called *Awakenings* about the hundreds of thousands of people stricken by encephalitis lethargica epidemic during and after WWI.

"This is good," Auden said, "but, if I may make a suggestion, your writing is too dry—too analytical."

"The subject is clinical."

"Yes, but I think you should write about this in a way that is beyond the clinical. Be metaphorical. Be mythical."[177]

With Auden's encouragement, Dr. Sacks took his advice and rewrote his manuscript, and in so doing, became known as the greatest science-storyteller of our time. In fact, he was referred to as the poet laureate of medicine. His books are considered medical literature. Published in 1973, *Awakenings* went on to inspire the 1982 play *A Kind of Alaska* by Harold Pinter and the 1990 Oscar-nominated film, *Awakenings* starring Robert De Niro and Robin Williams. He gave Auden the manuscript of *Awakenings*, and after reading it, Auden told him that he thought it was a masterpiece. The 1976 edition of *Awakenings* is dedicated to the memory of W.H. Auden.

Dr. Sacks visited Auden in Oxford in February 1973. It had been a beautiful day, so instead of taking a cab, he decided to walk. When he found Auden, he was standing there swinging a pocket watch.

"You're twelve and a half minutes late," Auden said.

He should have known better than to keep him waiting. Auden was obsessed with punctuality. He always arrived three hours early to the airport to catch his flights.[178]

Dr. Sacks said that before meeting Auden, he was insecure and had very little intellectual self-confidence. In fact, he was extremely shy in social situations, so much so, that as a young boy, he said that he could relate with inert gases, imagining them also as lonely, cut off, and yearning to bond.[179] However, after meeting Auden and taking that encouragement to heart, he became a different person. It had been the first time in his life that someone so special and influential had noticed him. Before that, no one had ever said such reassuring things to him, or had looked at him in such a positive light. Auden's encouragement forever changed him.

I know exactly how Dr. Sacks felt.

In the late 70s, I thought I was having a heart attack. I went to my doctor who sent me for a stress test.

"It's not your heart," he said. "It's your esophagus. I'm going to send you to a pathologist at Lenox Hill Hospital."

The pathologist performed an esophageal test where he put a scope down my throat and took a biopsy. A few days later, he called me back with the results.

"I'm afraid it's cancer," he said. "I'm going to send you to a surgeon."

The surgeon he referred me to laid out the whole ghastly operation.

"I'll cut you open and take part of your esophagus, but first we'll do chemotherapy to try and get rid of the cancer. Then we'll operate."

As he drew a diagram of the operation on a legal pad, I held up my hand.

"Wait just a minute. You're cutting out this and cutting out that. It looks as though I'll come out of this operation three inches shorter than when I go in. I want a second opinion."

Morty volunteered for some sort of testing at New York Hospital in the urology department, so he got to know the Head of Urology, so he spoke to that doctor about my condition.

"You're in luck," the doctor said. "The new president of Cornell Medical School at New York Hospital is Dr. David Skinner. He's an esophageal surgeon and has just been assigned here as president.

"I'm going to get in touch with Dr. Skinner and make an appointment for you to see him. Let's make a list of questions to ask him."

"Yeah, like does he have any living patients."

I met with Dr. Skinner and he performed the same test. Afterwards, we met in his office.

"I don't believe you have cancer," he said. "Not yet anyway. I can see where the pathologist misdiagnosed you. He mistook it for cancer because you do have suspect cells, precancerous cells, but they are not yet cancerous. They're right on the verge."

He showed me pictures of the cells.

"You have Barrett's Syndrome which is a serious condition caused by years of acid reflux in the lower part of the esophagus. The repeated exposure to the stomach acids cause the normal lining of the esophagus to change into tissue that more resembles the lining of the intestine. The cells become precancerous and can lead to cancer if not treated in time. You caught it in time."

"Thank God," I said.

"90% of the people who have Barrett's Syndrome and don't treat it get cancer. 90% of those people tend to be men. Seldom women. You're the 10% of the 10%."

"Lucky me. So, I don't need an operation?"

"No. In the first place, we would have never given you chemotherapy when you're perfectly healthy just to wear you down and then operate on you. If anything, it would be done the opposite way. But that's not what we're talking about."

"What happens now?"

"You have to completely change your diet. You have to give up your martinis, caffeine, spices—all of it."

"Okay."

"We're going to have to monitor you. You'll have to come back periodically and redo this test."

"I don't care if I have to do this test every other day for the rest of my life."

"If you had gone through the treatment that had been suggested, I'm afraid you would have had serious complications."

"Complications?"

"There is a very good chance you would have died."

"Huh."

I was retested every month for a while, then every three months, then every six months. And I stuck to that diet for many, many years.

I find that whenever I listen to my gut, my inner voice, things turn out all right for me. But when I ignore that inner voice, things tend to go badly. I'm so thankful I listened to my gut and got that second opinion. And I'm so grateful to have had Dr. Skinner take care of me. He was a great doctor. And as it turned out, he saved my life.

W.H. Auden
Courtesy of the San Diego History Center
© San Diego History Center, Di Gesu Collection

Chapter Twenty-Seven

In heaven, all the interesting people are missing.
— Friedrich Nietzsche

I t was Friday, September 28, 1973. Auden had just given a poetry reading at the Palais Palffy in Vienna for the Austrian Society for Literature. He had closed up their summer home in Kirchstetten for the season and booked two rooms at the Altenburgerhof Hotel for the night before his flight to England the next morning. One room was for Chester, the other for himself. They wanted to spend a few nights together in Vienna before they went their separate ways again for the winter. Auden wasn't looking forward to returning to Oxford. Chester hadn't attended the reading, but rather spent the night out on the town with a few Greek friends. After the reading, Auden headed straight to the hotel and went to bed.

He had asked Chester to come to his hotel room and wake him in the morning so he wouldn't miss his flight. Chester tried to enter the room, but the door was locked. To anyone else, that would seem quite normal, but Chester knew that Auden never locked his door at the Altenburgerhof.[180] He knocked on the door and called Auden's name, but there was no answer. Fearing something terrible had happened, he rushed to the front desk and had the manager come with the key. When they opened the door, they found the hotel room in complete disarray as though he had been living there for months. Chester took one look at Auden, lying on his left side, and knew right away that he was dead. His body was cold and still. Chester remembered that many years before, Auden jokingly predicted that he would die in "a *louche* (disreputable) hotel."[181] Sometime between 9:00 p.m. and the early hours of that rainy morning, Auden died in his sleep. He was 66 years old.[182] The medical examiner concluded that Auden had died of hypertrophy of the heart, which is the abnormal enlargement or thickening of the walls of the heart.[183]

"According to the amount of rigor, he died very early this morning," the medical examiner said.

"No," Chester protested, "he died on Friday night. Wystan never would have died after midnight."[184]

The world heard the sad news of Auden's death on Sunday, September 30th. His friends later recalled that Auden had often told his spirit that when it was time for it to go, that it needed to "bugger off quickly." And so, it did.

The Dean and Chapter of Westminster Abbey suggested that his ashes be buried there, but Auden had specifically wanted to be laid to rest in the village churchyard in Kirchstetten. Even though he wasn't Catholic, he had been a congregant there for many years. His brother, John, friends, scholars, writers, artists, and representatives from England, Austria, and the United States came to the funeral. The small garden was packed with TV cameras and newspaper reporters.

It was Thursday, October 4th, and one of those at the funeral that crisp, clear morning was his writer friend, Charles Osbourne. Auden had recently gone to London and had lunch with Charles who remembered him being bubbly and looking healthier than he had been in a long time. He spoke happily about his youth and the good old days. A few weeks later, Charles found himself in Austria standing at the edge of a hole in the ground "flinging his spadeful of earth onto Auden's coffin."[185]

Before the funeral, Charles made his way to Auden's house. Chester and six or seven others were sitting in the living room/dining room picking at food from plates that had been left by well-wishers. Chester sat and stared blankly at the walls and babbled incoherently. After a few glasses of wine, Charles went to the kitchen for a glass of water and was startled to find the coffin containing Auden on the kitchen table. He went to the other room to say goodbye to Chester and happened to see out the window that Auden's coffin was being loaded into the hearse. The village brass band followed his body to the cast-iron cross in the Kirchstetten churchyard.[186]

"I want all film people with their microphones, photographers, and the press to leave the garden, also any other person not invited to be in the house to go, please," Chester said. "There's something I have to do."[187]

Once all the reporters had gone, Chester positioned himself beside a gramophone.

"Wystan wanted a certain piece of music by Wagner, *Siegfried's Funeral March* from *Die Götterdämmerung*, to be played at his funeral," Chester said. "So, I'd like you all to stand while we play it."[188]

The needle found its groove in the album, and Wagner's low and mournful horns, oboes, and bassoons, pounding drums, and haunting strings came pouring out of the horn. There wasn't a dry eye in the place.

Auden had undoubtedly met thousands of wonderful, fascinating, and handsome men throughout his life, but it was Chester who held his heart from that spring afternoon in 1939 right up until that very last night in Vienna in the autumn of 1973.

It was only after Auden's death that Chester realized the depth of what he had lost. He had not only lost his friend, his meal ticket, his safety net, but most important, Chester realized that he would never again be worshipped by anyone as completely and without judgement as he was by Auden. The hard truth was, despite his many friends and his lovers, Chester was all alone in this world.

"I have lost my criterion," Chester said.

He returned to Greece and spent the night in an ouzo-fueled stupor. He developed a bleeding ulcer, gained weight, and lost hair. He flew to England to Westminster Abbey for the unveiling of a memorial stone to Auden in Poet's Corner. Chester stood, lost and alone, head bowed—a shadow of the man he once was—that many of Auden's friends hardly recognized him.[189]

The following year, he came back to Austria and sold the Kirchstetten house to the maid for next to nothing and went back to Greece. On January 17, 1975, Chester was home with two close friends: the first was a master carpenter who had just come back from Libya, and the second was a soldier named Vassilis who was home on leave one last night. On the morning of January 18th, Vassilis went to Chester's bedroom to say goodbye before returning to the barracks. He found that Chester had died in his sleep. He was only 54 years old.

Vassilis remained at Chester's side until the paramedics arrived and answered all official questions. In doing so, he was reported as missing on base. When he returned, he was arrested and spent twenty-four hours in jail and was confined to his barracks. Nevertheless, he was given time off to attend Chester's funeral. Chester was laid to rest in a Jewish cemetery in Athens. Before the funeral, several friends gathered for lunch and listened to Chester's favorite music together.[190]

Although none of his family attended the funeral, that wasn't unusual. It would have been very difficult for them to travel halfway around the world on such short notice. Besides, Chester hadn't been close to his family for years, because they didn't accept his lifestyle.[191] Chester had been the sole beneficiary of Auden's estate, but he himself had willed everything he owned to Auden and had not updated his will after Auden's death. Therefore, Chester's closest living relative, in this case his father, inherited Auden's entire estate.

Many who knew the two of them imagined that Auden found Heaven simply unbearable without Chester, so he called him up to be with him. Auden's and Chester's relationship endured to the very end of their lives, because they had many shared interests, they genuinely enjoyed collaborating together, and they knew each other right down to the ground. And they truly loved one another. Beyond sex. Beyond poetry.

I had followed Auden's life nearly all of my life, and I mourned his death. All that day, I thought about the afternoon he and I spent together in Stewart's Cafeteria, discussing poetry and him encouraging me, both as a budding poet and as a young woman trying to find her way in the world. I couldn't help but recall his poem *Funeral Blues*.

Funeral Blues

Stop all the clocks, cut off the telephone,
Prevent the dog from barking with the juicy bone.
Silence the pianos and, with muffled drum,
Bring out the coffin. Let the mourners come.

Let aeroplanes circle moaning overhead
Scribbling in the sky the message: "He is dead!"
Put crepe bows around the white necks of the public doves.
Let the traffic policemen wear black cotton gloves.

He was my north, my south, my east and west,
My working week and Sunday rest,
My noon, my midnight, my talk, my song.
I thought that love would last forever; I was wrong.

The stars are not wanted now; put out every one.
Pack up the moon and dismantle the sun.
Pour away the ocean and sweep up the wood.
For nothing now can come to any good.[192]

I was terribly sad that Auden was gone, but the night sky seemed to blaze with intensity now that one of their brightest stars had come home at last.

Chapter Twenty-Eight

Auden had a reoccurring dream in which he had to catch a train, and that everything depended upon it. The world would end if he didn't catch that train. All sorts of obstacles got in his way, and he grew more and more anxious. Finally, he reached the platform, but saw the steam rise from the train's smokestack as it pulled out without him. He was too late. And he would wake up with an orgasm and a smile on his face.[193]

I've had the same reoccurring dream about a train for as long as I can remember. Lately, I've been dreaming this dream more and more frequently, but I can't say that I ever woke up with the same elation as Auden. My dream starts with me sitting on a train. I never see myself get on, but rather, I'm already seated, and the train is moving. Sometimes I'm alone in the car, and sometimes there are people there, but I never interact with them. I never know where I'm going, but I'm not afraid. I always wake up before I get to where I'm supposed to go. I have no idea what it means. Maybe I was a conductor in a former life.

One time, Morty and I took a course about dreams at Queens College. This woman we met there talked about a dream she had.

"I imagine these dreams come from the universal consciousness," she said.

"No, they have to come from your own subconscious," I said. "Whatever you dream comes from your head and your experiences."

I gave her an example. We were having a group of people over for dinner. Steven called and said that he had to be in New York for work and he was going to bring Amelia over and have us watch her for the night.

"No, I'm sorry, but I can't watch her. I have to get ready to host twelve people for dinner party, and I simply won't have time to watch her. I'll be cooking and getting the house ready."

"Okay, but you're going to lose her."

So, I said to that woman, "That night, I dreamt that Morty, Amelia, and I were walking in the park, and all of a sudden, I couldn't find Amelia. I kept calling her name, but I just couldn't find her. She was lost. So, you see what I mean about dreams coming from your own head."

Since I met that woman, I have heard and read many other people that say that when we dream or meditate we somehow tap into the universal consciousness. That might explain how some people who invent things, like the Wright Brothers, or Leonardo da Vinci, or have a talent that far surpasses their years such as Mozart may acquire that talent or idea. Paul McCartney said that he dreamt the song *Yesterday*. He woke up with that tune in his head and went straight to the nearby upright piano and played it.

Likewise, there have been people in history who had the same idea for an invention at the same time, but they don't know each other nor are they in the same location. Take, for example, George Westinghouse, Thomas Edison, Nikola Tesla. These men all had similar ideas about electricity setting up the war of currents or the battle of currents which refers to a series of events surrounding the introduction of competing electric power transmission systems in the late 1880s and early 1890s. They weren't collaborating, so what was it that brought the same idea into their heads at the very same time?

I have always been fascinated with Leonardo da Vinci. In fact, I took a course on da Vinci. I am convinced that he was superhuman—that he really was an exceptional being from another time. Everything he did was above and beyond our reach at that time. I believe that there is a highly-evolved race from the future among us here on earth. There have been other geniuses, of course—Albert Einstein, Stephen Hawking, and Galileo just to name a few. They had specialties, like physics or mathematics, but couldn't paint or sculpt, for example. Leonardo da Vinci was not only a master whose genius spanned many varied disciplines, but he also invented so many things. Here are just a few: the helicopter, the tank, the machine gun, the flying machine, the revolving bridge, the giant crossbow, the triple barrel cannon, the robotic knight, the parachute, scuba gear, the paddle boat, the self-propelling cart, and the anemometer, which is an instrument that measures wind speeds.[194]

The first time Morty and I visited Florence, Italy, which is still my favorite city, we decided to take a half-day guided tour just to get an overall feel of the city. We knew then and there that we would be back. Fortunately for us, our guide that day was also an art historian who took us to the Uffizi Gallery.

"Why are there so few works by Leonardo da Vinci here?" I asked.

"Leonardo was first and foremost a scientist who also painted."

We stood before Leonardo's painting *Annunciation* which depicts the angel Gabriel who was sent by God to announce to the Virgin Mary that she would conceive and give birth to a son named Jesus who would be called the Son of God.

"Leonardo was only twenty-three when he painted this," the guide said. "Not only do we see the detail of the Tuscan trees he studied—the oaks, pines, and cypresses, but take a look at these wings. Leonardo was an engineer who understood the mechanics of flight."

He motioned to me to get closer to the painting.

"Senora, I want you to take a close look at the wings of the Archangel Gabriel. They aren't like anything else you'll see in other masters' paintings. He studied the mechanics and aerodynamics of wings. These wings are so anatomically correct, they could fly."

The wings of Leonardo's *Annunciation* angel are ingeniously designed. They appear alive. Leonardo wasn't a religious man, but like many painters, he made his living off of commissioned pieces, most of them for the church. But when he painted, he took the opportunity to try out his greatest invention—the flying machine. From the 1480s to the early 1500s, he designed flying machines with complicated systems of pulleys and levers and bat-like wings.[195] He often purchased caged birds and set them free. He was also a vegetarian who detested violence and war. For Leonardo, having wings and taking flight was his lifelong dream. He pictured a future where humans would have the ability to fly, to be released from the earthly shackle of their gravity and to be free.

Morty and I ended up travelling to the town of Vinci just to see where he came from. They have a museum there dedicated to him with all his inventions and working models. They have coins that he minted. Even examples of his writing. Leonardo invented his own form of shorthand, but he also wrote in mirror writing starting on the right side of the page writing backwards to the left. You need to hold a mirror up to the paper in order to read it. When he wrote a letter or papers intended for others to read, he wrote regularly, but all his own personal papers and documents were written in mirror writing. People who saw him write and paint say that he was left handed, so there are theories that he wrote right to left to keep his hand clean from dragging it across the paper.[196] But then why write the text backwards? Was he being cryptic or clever? One thing is for certain: the man was a supergenius.

Throughout our human existence, we've gone through intellectual cycles. Look at the artistic and mathematical achievements of ancient Greece, the incredible minds that engineered and built the Egyptian and Mayan pyramids, and the creation of the Mayan calendar, and those who built Machu Picchu, and those people who sailed their ships across the sea guided by their knowledge of the cosmos. Then the pendulum swung back to an age, the Middle Ages for example, where our knowledge and understanding retracted. Then the pendulum vacillated back to that culturally-enlightened awakening period during the Renaissance. I think our human evolution, while pushing forward, is not linear. It's more like a sine wave—it's always moving forward, but it has its ups and downs.

Chapter Twenty-Nine

On June 12, 1981, Morty and I went to dinner with our son, Dan, and his friend, Vivian. We were celebrating our 45th wedding anniversary. After we ordered drinks, Vivian commented on our marriage.

"You've been married forty-five years," she said. "That's amazing. In all that time, had you even thought of divorce?

I smiled and said, "Divorce, no. Murder, often."

In 1984, Steven decided to take a year's sabbatical and holed up in our Mohegan house. Amelia was five years old, so we put heat in the house so it could be used year-round. I have no idea what possessed me to write this limerick:

1984

Steven's Limerick

There is a young doc named Stephen
Whose life is very uneven
He travels so much

That he keeps in touch
By arrivin' just as he's leavin'

I smoked nearly my entire life until one specific day in 1984. Just as I can remember the exact day that I started to smoke, I can remember the exact day that I quit. My granddaughter, Amelia, was five. A year before that, Steven and Anne had taken the girls to Hawaii because he had some kind of work engagement. They were in their hotel room on the twentieth floor. Anne went out to the balcony and came back inside.

"Steven, I smell smoke. I think the hotel is on fire."

He called to the front desk and they said that, yes, the hotel was on fire. Steven grabbed Elizabeth, who was an infant, and Amelia, took them both in his arms, and ran down all twenty flights of stairs, holding them tightly the whole time. The panic that he must have felt transferred itself to Amelia. After that, she was terrified not only of fire, but also of anyone smoking.

We were all together in a hotel in Philadelphia, and she saw a sign that read "Exit," and she said to me, "I know that sign. That's for if there's a fire." And then she asked me, "Nana, are you smoking?"

The look on that precious girl's face and her concern for me was all it took. It was so important to her that I not smoke, that I decided right then and there to quit smoking.

Although I no longer smoked, I still enjoyed my cocktails. I never took drugs, though. Auden, on the other hand, tried both marijuana and LSD. He said that after smoking pot once, it gave him a distorted, confused feeling that was the exact opposite of the feeling he got with alcohol. He said he would repeatedly try to start a sentence, but then couldn't remember how they began.

Auden took LSD once under a doctor's supervision. Why a doctor would agree to this is beyond me, but his physician came to his

St. Mark's Place apartment at 7:00 a.m. and gave him a dose. He felt dizzy and slightly detached from his body. Auden doubted that the drug would have much of an effect on him because he was "completely pickled in alcohol anyway."

At about 10:00 a.m. when the drug was supposed to have been at its most potent, the two of them walked down to the corner coffee shop to have breakfast. Auden looked up from his ham and eggs out the window and saw a vision.

"And then it happened! I thought I saw my mailman doing a strange dance with his arms and legs and mail sack. Well, I never see my mailman before noon—so I was very impressed by the results of the LSD."

The following day, the angry mailman showed up at Auden's apartment.

"What's the matter with you?" he asked Auden. "I saw you in the coffee shop yesterday, and I waved at you and jumped up and down to catch your eye, but you looked right at me and didn't even give me a nod."

Auden came to the conclusion that drugs weren't for him. From then on, he vowed that he belonged only to the "cigarette-alcohol culture, not the drug culture."[197]

My drink of choice back then was a very dry Tanqueray martini with olives. You didn't even need Vermouth. I heard the best way to make a martini is to pour a capful of Vermouth into a metal shaker filled with ice, immediately pour the Vermouth out, then add the gin to the shaker. You only need enough Vermouth to coat the ice—just a drop or two to contemplate its mysteries. Sheer heaven.

I haven't had a martini in years. I may have an occasional glass of wine with dinner, but I don't dare have a martini now. All I need is to get tipsy, topple over, and break a hip. But the thought of an ice-cold martini still puts a smile on my face. Morty never smoked or drank, but that never stopped me. Who says a couple has to share everything?

I once read a book about Eleanor Roosevelt. When her grandson was fourteen, she took him to London. I thought that was a wonderful idea. So, in 1989 when Amelia was ten, I told Steven that I wanted to take her to London. I figured it would be easy because of the language and similar culture, so I'd be able to manage.

"Well, you're not going to take Amelia without Anne."

"Okay, I'll take Anne."

"Well, you can't take Anne and leave Elizabeth.'

"Okay, I'll take her, too."

"You're going to leave Dad at home?"

"Okay, I'll take Dad."

So, the five of us flew to London. I thought for sure Steven would join us, too, but he stayed home. He updated his passport, just in case he had to leave at a moment's notice to come and rescue them.

We had a great time. I was a travel agent at the time for Consolidated Tours which was an offshoot of American Travel Abroad. I took them to Stonehenge by train because I wanted them to have the experience of riding on a train. We went to Bath by bus, Madame Tussauds, and the British Museum, and to three plays. One was some electric thing on roller skates, and *Cats*, and a musical comedy called *Me and My Girl.*

One of those days, we decided to have lunch, not in a Public House, but a proper restaurant. Several boys sat together at a table, and as we passed, they took one look at Amelia and applauded. She was mortified, but we howled with laughter.

Amelia wrote me a letter about a year ago thanking me for all the things we did for her and her sister growing up.

"I'll never forget that trip to Europe," she wrote. "Never."

Me, Elizabeth, Amelia, Anne, and Morty at Stonehenge

I remember once when Amelia was about three, and Anne had come to the city for a visit with her before Elizabeth was born. My friend Sadie came over to my house to join us for lunch at Bloomingdale's. Sadie took one look at Amelia and said, "You're gorgeous. Look at your hair!"

While we were at lunch that afternoon, the waitress stopped and smiled at Amelia.

"You're so cute," the waitress said.

Amelia gave her a look. "I'm gorgeous, look at my hair."

It's lovely to see that both my granddaughters are beautiful, both inside and out. And they still know how to make me laugh.

Me and Morty

Chapter Thirty

I'll love you, dear, I'll love you
Till China and Africa meet,
And the river jumps over the mountain
And the salmon sing in the street
— W. H. Auden, *As I Walked Out One Evening*

L ife changes in an instant. At 8:15 a.m. on a sunny Monday morning in August 1945, a woman very much like me stood in her kitchen in Hiroshima, Japan, fixing breakfast while her son, like my son Steven, played beside her on the floor. She had no idea that an American B-29 bomber named the *Enola Gay* flying above the city had released a five-ton bomb, the first atom bomb, and that at 8:16 a.m., she and her son, along with 80,000 other souls, would be no more. On another perfectly blue-skied Tuesday morning in September 2001, men and women started their day on the 96th floor of the North Tower of the World Trade Center in New York City. They turned on their computers, checked their emails, and poured their cups of coffee in office kitchens when American Airlines flight 11 obliterated floors 93-99. On a chilly evening in September 1947, a drunk driver travelling southbound on the Palisades Parkway drifted into the northbound lane and instantly killed four precious members of my family.

June 18, 1991—just an ordinary rainy Tuesday night. Morty and I invited our friend Sadie to come to the theater with us. Her husband had died a few years before, and I tried not to let her be alone. We often had dinner together, and whenever we went to the theater, we invited Sadie to come along. The three of us went to see *The Prisoner of Second Avenue*. Afterwards, we dropped Sadie off at her house, and we drove home.

"I'll be up in a minute," Morty said shaking his umbrella. "I just want to go downstairs to the office and check my messages."

I went upstairs, washed up, and got ready for bed. I slipped on my nightgown, and Morty joined me in the bedroom. He went straight for the air conditioner and turned it on high.

"Morty, what are you doing? It's cold in here. It figures, when you're hot I'm cold, and when you're cold, I'm hot."

He stood beside the bed. "Stop it," he said.

And just then, he fell onto his knees and his torso flopped onto the bed. He remained face down on the bed.

"Get up. Morty, if you don't get up, I'm going to call 9-1-1."

I immediately knew something was horribly wrong. Morty wasn't a joker. In fact, he had a terrible sense of humor, so I know he would have never fooled around about something like this. I turned him over and laid him onto the floor so I could do what I thought was CPR.

He never moved, so I called 9-1-1 from the bedroom phone. We had two phones with two different extensions—one for the house and the other for Morty's office. I picked up the other phone and called Sadie, then Dan in Philadelphia, then Steven in Colorado, then Doris and Bernie. I stayed on the phone with 9-1-1 until I heard the ambulance outside. I ran down and let the paramedics in.

What happened next, I still can't explain. I walked to the living room and sat down on the sofa. Sadie, Doris, and Bernie had arrived. Sounds and voices fluttered down the stairs from the bedroom, but I sat calmly in the living room. It was as if all of this was happening to someone else, and I was simply watching from a distance. All I can say is that I shut down.

As the paramedics came downstairs with Morty on their stretcher, I think I remember asking, "Where are you going?", but I have no recollection of where they told me. They could have said the hospital or the morgue.

"I'll go with them," Bernie said.

"Get his ring," I said. "It has an MD on it."

I don't know why I said that. Maybe in the back of my mind I knew he was dead. Bernie left and a little while later came back with Morty's ring. Bernie might have also given me the rest of his personal effects—wallet, keys, pocket change—I don't remember.

As I thought, Morty was dead. He was 77 years old. We had been married 55 years. He hadn't been sick as far as I know, and he never mentioned that he was feeling off in any way. As it turned out, he died of sudden cardiac death (SCD). Unlike a heart attack where blood is blocked from reaching the heart, people who suffer SCD die without any warning because of an electrical malfunction in the heart. The heart stops pumping and seconds later, the person loses consciousness and has no pulse. Death follows immediately.[198]

Life changes in an instant. One moment, Morty was walking across the bedroom floor, and the next moment he was gone. Years later, I read *The Year of Magical Thinking* by Joan Didion where her husband dropped dead at dinner, and it made me think of Morty dying so suddenly. To this day, I buy that book for people I know who have experienced a loss.

"Would you like us to stay with you tonight?" Doris asked. "Or you can come home with us."

"No."

"You shouldn't be alone tonight," Sadie said. "It's no trouble for me to stay here."

"I'm fine, really."

I knew that Dan had to make arrangements for someone to watch his adopted son, Bill, and he would be there first thing in the morning. Steven and Anne made phone calls and got everyone together and would be in New York a day or two.

"If you're sure," Doris said. "Call us if you need anything, and we'll come right over."

I walked them to the door and watched them leave. Again, it was as though they had just come to dinner any other night. I went upstairs and went to bed. Forget the fact that my husband was dead and that he had died right there on that bed. I was so completely disassociated from the experience, it was as though I had watched a movie, and none of it was real.

Dan came the following morning, and we planned the funeral. We decided to have Morty cremated. For obvious reasons, given the Holocaust, Jewish Law forbids cremation, but we weren't very religious. Besides, that's what Morty wanted.

The funeral was held at some place on Union Turnpike in Queens. The same thing happened to me during the funeral as had happened at the house. I completely shut down. I greeted people, watched them hug one another, and listened to them speak about all of Morty's accomplishments while I sat and listened. Nothing was connecting. It was as though I had stepped right into a movie theater and was watching everything unfold on a screen. I wasn't crying. I wasn't numb. Our good friend, Sid Druce, must have noticed my unusual behavior, because he came over to me, sat down next to me, and took my hand in his.

"It's okay to cry," Sid said.

I did the same thing when my mother died. When my father called me to say my mother fell down and wouldn't wake up, Morty and our friends went into the bathroom, but I stayed by myself in the living room and sat down on the sofa. I never moved from the sofa when they all gathered in the kitchen to discuss what to do. I assume the paramedics came at some point, but I have no memory of them. Just as with Morty, I shut down.

After the funeral, many of our friends and family drove up to the house in Mohegan and sprinkled Morty's ashes in the flower bed along the front of the house. I wanted to put them there because that place meant a lot to both of us. Every year, Morty and I worked on those flowers together, and its beauty always gave us a sense of pride.

Everyone took some of the ashes and planted them in the garden—all except Elizabeth. It was too emotional for her, so she stood by and watched.

"It's okay," I said. "You don't have to if you don't want to."

I went back to the Queens house to contact all of Morty's patients and refer them to other doctors, then I closed that house up and spent the summer in Mohegan with Anne and the girls.

A few years later, Bernie died, and Doris had his ashes buried in the same flower bed. Then a few years later, Dan's black lab died, and his ashes were buried in the flower bed. After that, my friend's husband's ashes went into the flower bed. When my friend, Jo Grellong's father died, she asked me if he could go in the flower bed, too, but his wife vehemently objected.

"There's no way I'm going to put him in there with the dog!"

Our flower bed was sentimental for me, and it reminded me of another very special flower garden. I had six girlfriends growing up in the Colony, and we were as close as siblings. The seven of us did everything together. In the fall of 1930, Ruth Manson, one of the seven, was killed in a car accident. She was only fourteen years old.

Ruth's parents printed up a book of Ruth's poems for the six of us girls. One of the founders of the Colony, Harry Kelly, wrote a Tribute to Ruth in the front of the book:

Whether it is better to die young when one is in the full bloom of what seems a promising life, or to live on to become disillusioned, and perhaps cynical, is a question which cannot be answered once for all. Reading the dreams, thoughts and frequently keen observations of Ruth Manson one can be sure that those who knew her and loved her are the poorer by her tragic death. What she would have become had she lived it is difficult to say, but that she was thinking and groping toward understanding can hardly be doubted. She did not appear to be one of those prodigies who are acclaimed in youth only to grow up to accept the cowardice, falsehood and injustice that surround us because we are too timid or too indolent or lack initiative to defy them. Courage and initiative, like cowardice and sloth, if cultivated can become habits and Ruth started in the right direction.

My own recollection of this child—she was only fourteen—stands out vividly as I read and reread these random thoughts of hers. Coming to the Colony one day in the early summer of 1930 I met her with her sister on the Colony bus. Not having seen them for some time, I was a bit puzzled as to who these rosy cheeked girls could be. When I finally recognized them, I asked jokingly at what druggist's shop they had bought the beautiful bloom on their cheeks. For a moment they were silent, and then Ruth answered shyly, "We got it at the Colony." The reply pleased me more than I can tell, for I thought: Surely here is compensation for those who labored to bring forth the little community known as Mohegan Colony. Did we not visualize a group of such children full of joy, of living, growing and making a new and beautiful place in the Westchester Hills, a community to be personified in the quick wit, glowing cheeks and abundant health of our children? It was such as she who loomed large in the minds of those who dreamed of happy, healthy children living in a beautiful environment in comradeship and symbolizing the new day. And now she of the quick wit and lovely cheeks has gone and left even me, who saw her but seldom, with a feeling of sadness that one so young, so full of promise, one seeking after truth—that rare and beautiful thing— has departed, and all that remains is a memory; but a memory full of hope and beauty.

After Ruth's parents presented us girls with the remembrance book, they made arrangements for us to plant a garden in her name beside the school. It was called Ruth's Garden, and it was filled with sunflowers and tulips and daisies. A sundial was placed in the middle of the garden. Here I am planting Ruth's Garden.

I'd like to share one of Ruth's prolific and foreboding poems called *Sunset*:

Sunset

How like a sunset is death!
With each sublime sunset are lost one thousand lives,
When one dies who is young, the sunset holds a sorrowful
                                                    beauty.
When one dies who is hoary with age, the sunset is lengthy and
                                                    weary.
When one who has led a drab life dies, with a dreary dullness
                                        the sun sets.
When one who has led a joyous life dies, a glorious golden
                        sunset passes from earth and drops to China
                                        and beyond.

Tennyson wished at his death a calm peaceful sunset.
But not so Browning who wished his death like a fiery
                                        flaming ball,
not gracefully cushioning itself in the blue hills but
struggling down, half loath to leave this world.

Whenever I see sunflowers and tulips and daisies, I remember my
dear friend, Ruth Manson, her resplendent spirit, and the garden we
planted in her name with love.

Ruth Manson, aged 13

Chapter Thirty-One

After spending the summer in the country after Morty died, I went back to work in the travel agency in the fall. The agency was located in the Fisk Building on the corner of 57th Street and 8th Avenue. Every Wednesday, Morty used to drive in to the city, because he worked at Flower Hospital which was built by the New York Medical College on Fifth Avenue and 106th Street. He helped found the mental retardation clinic there which was one of the first clinics in the country devoted to the care, treatment, and rehabilitation of the people with mental retardation and their families. I was so proud of the work he did. And every Wednesday at the end of the day, he would pick me up at 57th Street and 8th Avenue. I stood at the corner and he would drive around, pull up to the curb, and I would hop in, and we'd go home.

After he died, each Wednesday after work, I would stand on the corner and wait for him to pick me up. I would watch the cars come around the corner and look for Morty in our car.

Eventually, I took the bus home. I stood on that corner every Wednesday for months. I knew he wasn't coming, but it was something I had to do.

I ended up going to a support group for women who had lost

their husbands. It was out in Great Neck, and it consisted of twelve women, almost all of them Jewish and living in Great Neck. It was run by a woman who was a social worker or psychologist. I certainly don't think she was a psychiatrist. She herself had lost her husband. She told us that after her husband died, she went with her mother to their country club for lunch. One of her mother's golfing buddies came up to her.

"I'm so sorry. I heard you lost your husband," she said.

"Careless of me, wasn't it?"

I told them about me standing on the corner waiting for Morty to pick me up.

"I know exactly what you mean," one of them said. "I spent hours scrubbing the stair carpets thinking, if they were clean enough, he'd come back."

I found it interesting that half of the women's husbands had died after a long illness, and the other half of their husbands had died out of the blue like Morty.

"You had a chance to say goodbye," I said to the half who spent time with their dying husbands.

"But we never did," one of them replied. I watched as that half all nodded their heads. Even though only one of them said it, they all agreed.

I met with the group for about a year, but in the end, it didn't help me much. People grieve in their own way, and I just needed time to heal. I've since noticed that a lot of people are afraid to say that someone has died. I don't remember anyone saying, "Your husband is dead." Dead is such a final, brutal word. I suppose it's kinder or more hopeful to say that our loved ones have passed away, or that they were lost or gone. Maybe we use these nebulous terms because we want to believe that there's something more—that those who die before we do are not really gone, but just beyond the veil, and that one day, we will be reunited with them. Maybe it's our own fear of death that keeps us from facing the inevitable? After all, "died" sounds so final, as though there is nothing more. It's simply…over.

I'll tell you an interesting thing. I was in a dentist chair one time getting something done. I have no idea what, but I was in more pain than I had ever been in my life. And I closed my eyes, and I saw my mother and Morty standing next to each other just standing and looking at me. They weren't smiling or welcoming me to go anywhere with them. They were just standing there looking at me. I have often thought, where did that come from? If I ever want to fantasize about the afterlife, I can see them standing there.

Me and Normie

Nine months after Morty died, I ran into our friend, Normie Miller, at the post office in Mohegan. The next day, he phoned me and asked me to lunch. A few days later, he asked me to dinner. I told the women in the support group about this, and they all thought it was a bad idea.

"It's much too soon to start dating," many of them said.

"It's not like that," I said. "He's just an old friend from the Colony. We've known each other since we were children, and there's something special about having someone in your life that has known you that long. As for dating him, I'm not the least bit interested in him romantically or anyone else for that matter."

I wasn't lying. I truly had no intension of dating Normie, but he kept coming around. Lydia had died many years earlier, so I think it was nice for him to meet up with a long-time friend, too. He had a great sense of humor and made me laugh a lot, which was exactly what I needed at the time. Normie and I travelled together. We went to dinner, the theater, and the movies. In fact, we saw so many movies that he once told a friend that with me, he was at the movies every twenty minutes. We went on cruises and trips and travelled well together.

One time, we decided to eat steak at every one of the steakhouses in the city just to see which was the best. One of the steakhouses we tried was Sparks Steak House on East 46th Street. That was the site of the infamous mob murder of Paul Castellano like something right out of *The Sopranos*.

Constantino Paul (Big Paul) Castellano was the head of the Gambino crime family in New York, this country's largest Cosa Nostra family at the time. On the afternoon of December 16, 1985, protégé of Dellacroce, John (Teflon Don) Gotti and his underboss, Salvatore (Sammy the Bull) Gravano sat in a Lincoln sedan on the corner of East 46th Street and Third Avenue while their hit team positioned themselves outside the restaurant.

At around 5:30 p.m., Castellano and his underboss, Thomas (Tommy) Bilotti pulled up at a red light beside Gotti and Gravano.

"That's them," Gravano said.

Gotti picked up his walkie-talkie and told the hitmen to get into position.[199]

As soon as Castellano got out of the car, he was shot in the face. He collapsed onto the ground with his head, face up, on the passenger floor of the car. Bilotti was shot as he was getting out of the car and lay face up in a puddle of blood in the middle of 46th Street. Gotti and Gravano watched from their car across the street. As the men lay dead and bloodied in the street, Gotti drove slowly over to look at the bodies.[200]

Patrons inside thought they heard fireworks and were asked to leave the restaurant. A photographer took pictures of the scene not knowing who the dead men were. As a policeman approached him.

"You should just keep taking pictures," the cop said.

"I don't know who they are," the photographer said.

"It's the hit of the century."[201]

Of course, all this happened well before Normie and I started our best steak quest. As an aside, Sparks gets my vote for best steaks hands down. Despite the mob hit.

I lived in the Queens house during the week and drove up to the Colony to spend the weekends there. Normie was living in the Colony in his son Phillip's house. I gave Normie a key to my house so he could check on things when I wasn't there.

One stormy Sunday night, I drove back to Queens from Mohegan, opened the front door, and noticed that the hallway bathroom light was on.

"That's stupid of me. I left the light on."

I walked into the living room, and the air conditioner that had been in the window was on the desk. I thought *my God that storm was terrible. It blew the air conditioner out of the window.* I went upstairs and saw that my bedroom had been ransacked. I then realized that I hadn't left the bathroom light on. Whoever broke into the house pushed the air conditioner in and came in through the window. I had had an alarm system, but I forgot to turn it on that weekend.

They didn't take much—a few gold rings that had been out on the dresser. They didn't go into the closet or armoire or take any of the silver. I knew it was mostly likely kids up to a bit of mischief. Nevertheless, it was nerve racking being in the house by myself after that. I put a gate on the front door and replaced the old air condition-er with one that couldn't be pushed in, but I never felt comfortable being there by myself after that. It was lonely rambling around that big house by myself, but the break in was the last straw. I had lived in that house since 1945—nearly 50 years, but it was time to sell.

The people who bought the house were so nasty. They com-plained about this and they hated that.

"Look, if you don't like the house, don't buy it," I said.

"No, we'll take it," the man said.

At the closing, their lawyer paused before signing the contract.

"I did a walk through before I came here," he said. "You removed the book shelves in the living room and now the paint doesn't match."

I had had enough of these people. "The house hasn't been paint-ed in ten years. If they wait another ten years, it'll match."
I found a nice rent-stabilized apartment in Midtown a block away from Doris and five blocks from Grand Central so I could easily take the train north to Mohegan. Not long after, Normie called me with a chuckle in his voice.

"Guess where I am right now," he said.

"How would I know?"

"I'm at your country home."

"Is something wrong? Was there a break in?"

"No. Everything's fine. I'm living here."

"What do you mean you're living there? What happened to your son's house?"

"He told me I had to leave, because he wanted to rent it to his secretary."

I was furious. Of all the nerve. "So, you took it upon yourself to just move into my house without asking me?"

"I had nowhere else to go."

Before I could wrap my mind around what had happened, his other son, Matthew, phoned me.

"I want to live in your house, too," he said. "I'll rent the spare room and pay whatever my father is paying you."

"Paying me? Your father isn't paying me anything. You will not live in my house, and furthermore, when I die, I'm going to put it in my will that you aren't allowed to live there. So, get that idea out of your head. It's not happening."

Miffed, he convinced Normie to move out because, as he told his father, "It's clear we're not wanted!"

Normie then moved to the city and into my building and rented a studio apartment on my floor, right next door to me. After Normie moved out of the house in Mohegan, I decided to sell that, too. I couldn't keep it up. I spoke to Steven and Dan, and although neither of them wanted me to sell, they couldn't take it. Steven was living in Colorado, and Dan was in Philadelphia. It didn't make sense for them to have it. And it couldn't stay empty. It would just deteriorate. It was a very sad day when that house sold, but I will always have my happy memories. As Heraclitus said, "The only thing that is constant is change." Truer words were never spoken.

I paid $1000 a month for Normie's studio. He had worked for Social Security, and for some reason, he didn't get Social Security when he retired, but rather a government pension, and that wasn't much. It felt good to help him. I had the means, and in my mind, I was doing good for an old friend who was keeping me company.

I was completely aware that he and his family were taking advantage of me, but it was simply pitiful that all three of his wretched children would leave him homeless and penniless.

Phillip threw him out of the house, Hazel was in Detroit with her husband and never heard from nor seen, and Matthew was so lazy, he couldn't help him if he wanted to. Normie once told me that some music group opened a store in Westchester right outside of the Colony. He suggested to Matthew, who had never held a job, that he should ask about a position there. Matthew considered himself a DJ.

"It's music," Normie said. "It's what you like to do."

"I'm not going to be a slave to a company working 9 to 5!"

Instead of getting any job, Matthew scrounged around, and Normie gave him money—the money I gave Normie I might add.

Auden always paid Chester's way. Like Chester, Normie was helpless. He couldn't have provided for himself if wanted to, and his children would never have helped him out. Unlike Auden's love for Chester, I never loved Normie. We were fond of each other, but we were never in love. He asked me to marry him once, because he wanted my social security. I turned him down flat. Helping him out financially is one thing, but marriage? Not on your life. I had been married before, and once was enough. Besides, I knew that Normie had cheated on Lydia. As they say, once a cheater, always a cheater. Who needs that bologna?

Chapter Thirty-Two

Have you ever noticed when you read a good book in your teens, then read it again in your 20s or 30s, the book takes on new meaning? That same book read again in middle age, and yet again when grey hairs outnumber the rest, will reveal something brand new, because our life experiences allow us to reflect on that same story in a whole new way.

After a long pause of raising my sons and traveling with Morty, I thought about my poetry again. I found my old folder of poems in a desk drawer and reread them. In 1999 when I was 84 years old, I thought about the dead tree I had written about in *Blasphemy* when I was thirteen. I thought about how an 84-year-old might observe that same dead tree, which inspired me to write *Blasphemy 2*:

August 1999

Blasphemy 2

And still she stands
The leaves have fallen

One by one
Each taking a piece of the past
into oblivion
And still she stands
Bare and bereft
A creature of a long-gone era

What keeps her here?
A bit of green between her
blackened roots?
One trembling leaf clinging to
a twisted bough?
Not enough to hold her
here
When will she know?

March 2001

Vessel

I hold this vessel in
my hands
I have held it for
so very long.
The surface is cracked
and lined
And it is so heavy

But I cannot put
it down.

It is not quite full.
And even when it has
filled,
There will be so much
left not seen
not done
not said

Regretfully,
Regrettably.

Some of us who are old enough know exactly where we were when we heard that President Kennedy was shot. And when John Lennon was shot. Those who lived through 9/11 know exactly where we were when we heard about the Twin Towers. I was home that morning. I read the paper every morning after breakfast and never turn on the TV until after dinner, so I had no idea what had happened. Anne called me, and I could hear right away in her voice that something was terribly wrong.

"Turn on the TV," she said.

"What channel?"

"It doesn't matter."

It doesn't matter. The hair stood up on my arms. I turned on CNN and watched smoke billow out of the World Trade Center Building. The news anchors said they thought it might be a small plane that flew off course. A tragic accident. Then, on live television, we all saw the second plane fly into the adjacent tower. It was horrifying. And it was perfectly clear that it was no accident. I just couldn't believe my eyes. I watched as the South Tower collapsed at 9:59 a.m. The North Tower collapsed 29 minutes later.

I got dressed and went downstairs. I walked out my front door and to the corner. It was surreal. There were no cars on the street. No planes in the clear blue sky. It was eerily quiet. A sea of dust-covered people straggled up the middle of Second Avenue, staring blankly from white ash-covered faces. They could have been ghosts. One woman stopped near me.

"Where are you going?" I asked.

"I'm walking to Queens."

"Why don't you come upstairs with me and get cleaned up. I'll give you a wash cloth and towel so you can freshen up. I'll give you some tea or anything you like and then you can go on."

She shook her head. "I just want to keep walking. I have to get home."

I went back upstairs and spent the rest of the day locked in my apartment glued to the TV. Of the thousands of images taken on 9/11, AFP photographer Stan Honda took a photo of a woman named Marcy Borders who later became known as the Dust Lady. She was a 28-year-old Bank of America worker who fought her way down from the 81st floor of the North Tower after the first plane obliterated floors 93-99. She made it out of the building and was outside when the second plane struck the South Tower. She had been dressed for work, still wearing her pearls. The look of pain and shock and bewilderment on her face said it all.

After that horrible day, Marcy fell into a downward spiral of depression and addiction. She found peace and consolation after years of therapy and after hearing of Osama bin Laden's death. In August 2014, she was diagnosed with stomach cancer—something she was convinced was caused by the dust and ash from the Twin Towers. Marcy died on August 24, 2015. She was just 42 years old.[202]

Auden often wrote about the futility of war. His poem, *September 1, 1939*, resonated with so many people after 9/11. It was seen all

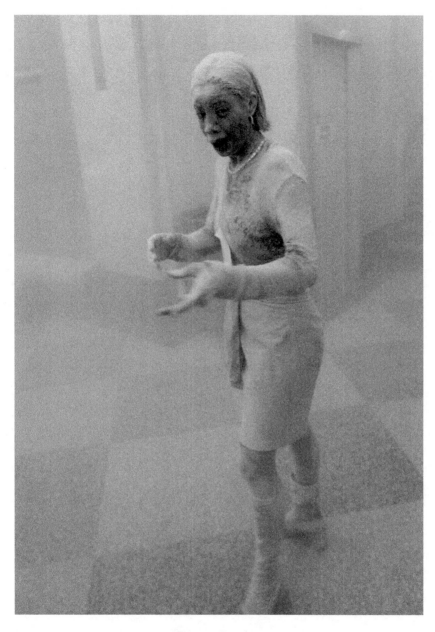

Marcy Borders
STAN HONDA/AFP/Getty Images

over the internet and read aloud at various memorial ceremonies. I think it spoke to people in part because it was written here in New York City. Auden was reflecting on the German invasion of Poland that day, but he touched on the collective suffering of all of humanity. And he mentions skyscrapers:

> Into this neutral air
> Where blind skyscrapers use
> Their full height to proclaim
> The strength of Collective Man,
> Each language pours its vain
> Competitive excuse;
> But who can live for long
> In a euphoric dream;
> Out of the mirror they stare,
> Imperialism's face
> And the international wrong. (lines 34-44)[203]

Chapter Thirty-Three

Normie and I had fun together. I know he enjoyed my company, but you wouldn't know it to look at him. He rarely smiled in photos. He was only happy while playing the violin. That was Normie. This limerick just came to me:

2004

Norman's Limerick

I know a man named Norman
Who has difficulty conformin'
His style of dress
Is often a mess
"But," says Norman, "I need no adornin'!"

I find that the older I get, the more I think about time—the time I spend with my family and friends, how much time I wasted worrying about things that simply didn't matter. How much time I have left. It's sad to read about people I know in the obituary, and yet, I'm still here.

2005

Time

Time is a moment suspended in space
And space is Time—it's our moment of grace
This moment will keep till the end of Time
One fraction I'll take of this moment—all mine
To have and to hold till death does me part of my time.

Time is in the mind
And my heart rules my head
A moment or a year you'll find
Is the same when we are dead

This year has been a moment
From which all time has passed
This moment from all time I've rent
And in my heart 'twill last

With sentiment prolific
And affection calorific
I beg leave to be specific
And call attention to the date

Were I not diplomatic
I would say in words emphatic
Though I'd hate to be dogmatic
That I won't be there too late.

According to Albert Einstein, the past, present, and future all exist simultaneously. He believed that time is actually relative and flexible. I get that. Our time here on Earth is determined by our position in the Solar System relative to the Sun and our planet's rotation. Einstein also believed that there is no distinction between the past and the future. Think about that for a minute. It's an interesting concept.

That same year I wrote this:

2005

Your world in the shape of an I

Your world in the shape of an I
Leaves horizons to you unbarred.
Your knowledge has limits on high,
By no fault is your mind left marred.

It must be weary for you indeed
To spend your life with such mortals as we.
So, my darling, I wish you Godspeed
To Valhalla where you can be free

Of such fetters imposed on you're here,
By those who respect not the wonder
Of having you with them, my seer.
Perhaps your peers will heed all your thunder!

August 2007

Reflection on my 91st birthday

When I am old:
I shall sit under a tree and read
my book and eat cherries
I shall sleep until noon and do
nothing all day
I shall not speak to anyone I
dislike, but I shall continue to
hold close those I love
I shall eat ice cream every day
I shall not ask how you are
unless I really want to know
I shall sit in the sun and
remember my youth, without
regrets
But not until I am old.

Auden often referred to the Almighty as "Miss G." I heard a joke one time about a guy who was in the hospital, and his heart stopped. He was clinically dead for about three minutes before the doctors were able to revive him. As soon as he awoke, his friend asked him what God was like.

"I don't think I should tell you."

"You have to. What was God like?"

"She was black."

If you live long enough, there comes a time when you do a lot of reflecting. What's life all about? How did I get here? Why am I still alive while others around me are dying or have already gone? What makes me so special that I'm still around? Are there lessons I have yet to learn? Or is it all random? Is there a God, and what is She like?

I don't have answers, and that's okay by me. Let the meaning of Life and Death unfold as it should. While on the journey, be kind to yourself. Love who you are as you age. Smile back at the wrinkles in the mirror. When you embrace the aging process and don't try to fight it, with any luck, you'll gain wisdom and patience and peace of mind.

Chapter Thirty-Four

My son Steven met his wife Anne while climbing in Colorado. He was on a mountain with a group of residents from the medical school. Anne was on a date with another man. She was somehow stuck or trapped when Steven's group came upon her. Her date might have gone for help or something, but he was nowhere to be seen, and Steven helped her down. He gave her his number and the rest they say is history.

Anne was one of the sweetest and kindest persons I have ever met. She and her family are from Colorado. She was born and raised in Durango, Colorado. Steven used to say that her father was a retired cowboy. The night before their wedding, we had a dinner party at the hotel in Denver, and I invited Anne's parents and grandparents. There was a head table set up for the parents and grandparents. I sat next to George, Anne's father. Somehow the conversation got to New England.

"What do you know about New England," I asked.

"We came from New England originally," George said. "We're direct descendants of John Alden."

If you know your history, John Alden was one of the crew

members of the 1620 voyage of the Mayflower. Instead of returning to England, he stayed at what became Plymouth Colony.

"Our mutual grandchildren will be direct descendants of John Alden, Dr. Dubovsky, and Abe Levy," I said.

"Don't worry, Annie isn't impressed either."

There were two big huge books that tracked their heritage in detail, but George and Anne's mother, Helene, kept getting divorced and remarried to each other, and somewhere along the way, they lost the books.

Anne became a Jehovah's Witness later in life. I don't think it was because she had some big religious epiphany. She was such a nice person that when a couple of women came to her door and asked to come in and talk to her, she let them in. Steven and the girls never converted or took it up. It was something that Anne did for herself. The girls weren't brought up Christian or Jewish. They respect both religions without a problem.

In 1994, Anne found a lump in her breast. Unfortunately, by the time she found it, her cancer was stage four and had spread to her bones. She underwent a double mastectomy and had chemotherapy and radiation treatments. It eventually spread to her brain and started radiation treatments there as well. She fought the disease for sixteen long years. Although she endured incredible pain throughout those dreadful years, she never lost her sweetness or sense of humor.

She finally succumbed in August 2010. Steven withdrew from the world. He was so terribly sad and lost. He locked himself inside the house and wouldn't go out. He became angry and mean.

A few years later, his tax attorney, Karen, stopped by the house one day to see him. She saw that the house was in shambles and took one look at Steven.

"I had never seen a more despondent human being in all my life," she later told me.

She came back, cleaned the house, and organized his life. She got him out and doing things again. She invited him to dinner and for bike rides.

Steven was a volunteer firefighter in his spare time and took Karen to one of the events.

"This is some date," Karen said.

"Oh, I didn't know this was supposed to be a date."

But that comment turned Steven's head. They began dating after that and have been happy together ever since. He came back to life with Karen. I truly believe she saved him, in every way a man can be saved.

A month after Anne passed away, Normie was rushed to the hospital with pneumonia. From there, he was sent to the Mary Manning Walsh Rehabilitation Home on York Avenue. It a was very nice place for him to get back on his feet and regain his strength, but whenever I visited him, he was quiet and mopey.

His daughter, Hazel, flew in from Detroit to visit Normie, but was rarely there. The day she arrived, she walked into Normie's room and saw that the nurse had written my name and telephone number down on the white board in case of an emergency.

"Why is your name up there? I want my name and number up there."

"Hazel, they're not going to call you in Detroit in case of an emergency."

"I don't care. I want my name there."

I called the nurse to come and add her name to the board. She stayed a few minutes but then gathered her things.

"I've got theater tickets for tonight, but I'll be back."

She never made it back that night. That was Monday night. As it turned out, she had tickets that evening, Tuesday evening,

Wednesday afternoon and evening, Thursday evening, Friday evening, and Saturday afternoon and evening. She was supposedly there to see her father, who was dying, but she spent most of her time at the theater.

Normie wasn't getting any better, and as usual, he wasn't happy.

"You're just laying here," I said. "You have to do what the nurses tell you and get better. "Why?"

"If you don't get better, you'll die."

"I want to die."

What do you say when someone says that? If someone wants to die, there's nothing anyone can do to convince them to live. Normie got his wish. He stayed in the facility for a few more weeks, then died there.

A day or two before he died, his children came to Normie's room and called me out into the hall.

"What can I help you with," I asked.

"We want to know everything that Dad has—all his money and his assets," Phillip said.

"What are you asking me for?"

"We want you to ask him and tell Hazel what he has."

I should have told them all to stick their request where the sun doesn't shine, but I asked Normie, and he wrote it all out. His entire estate was $35,000.00. I then told Hazel so they could fight about who was going to get what. As it turned out, there was no reason for me to ask him.

Phillip's daughter had already drawn up a will for Normie. They just didn't want to wait to know how much they would get.

A few days after Normie died, Hazel's husband came to my apartment and asked for the key to Normie's apartment.

"I want to go through Norman's books and papers," he said.

"Is there anything I can help you with?"

"No. I'm going to do it alone. We'll take it from here."

Imagine, they thought I was stealing money from Normie, when in fact, I was the one who paid for that apartment. I was the only one supporting him. All the furniture he had was my furniture he took out of my country house.

You can't please everyone. If you live long enough, you'll find that there are some people who will dislike you no matter what. And that's okay. Just wish them well and move on. After Normie died, I knew I would never hear from his children again. And that's fine with me.

Chapter Thirty-Five

Amelia married a wonderful man named Matt Rivara on June 2, 2012. She asked me to read my poem, *My Love*, at the wedding. A few years later, Elizabeth married an equally wonderful man named Peter Carreno, and I read that poem at her wedding as well. Afterwards, her new mother-in-law came up to me and introduced herself.

"Your poem made me cry," she said.

"It made me cry, too," said the woman next to her.

Afterwards, I was telling a friend of mine, Margaret Mahfood, about these women's responses to my poem.

"I don't understand why the poem made them cry," I said.

"I know why," Margaret said. "It's because there's such an outpouring of love in the poem."

The thing that struck me was that not only did these women cry when they heard my poem, Margaret understood perfectly why they cried. That's fascinating to me, because when I started writing the poem, I thought about my love for Morty, but it quickly grew away from my initial thoughts and became something much deeper. In other words, the poem took on a life of its own despite the kernel of inspiration.

That's the beauty and fascination of art for me. An artist might choose to paint the sky on a canvas a particular color because it pleased them or paint a tree or lake because they observed it on a hillside while vacationing in the country. Observers can look at that same tree or lake or sky and interpret something completely different than what the artist had in mind, because their moods or their life experiences allow them to take the painting and make it their own. Each person who reads an author's description of a scene in a novel will see that scene differently in his or her mind. Music, once composed and performed, will speak to the listener in a very unique and individual way. All art takes on a life of its own, and it becomes a living, breathing thing.

Those women's reactions to my poem that day got me to thinking again about how Auden had encouraged me to write all those years ago, reassuring me that I could be a great poet if I worked at my craft. I didn't believe him at the time, and I certainly wasn't about to contradict him, and that inspired me to write this poem:

2014

The Poet Said

The poet said
you, too can be
as great as I
greater, maybe.
Follow the path.
Do not stray.
No, no, there is
no other way.
I was afraid

to prove the great

    man wrong

and so

I took the other

    road.

We'll never know.

Actor, musician, and composer, Dudley Moore died on March 27, 2002 of pneumonia. He had suffered for years with a rare brain disease called Progressive Supranuclear Palsy (PSP), also called Steele-Richardson-Olszewski syndrome which had rendered him immobile. He had been holding the hand of his longtime friend, Rena Fruchter, when he died. Just before he passed away, Moore said, "I can hear the music all around me."[204]

What an incredible thought.

A few years ago, I read the book *Many Lives, Many Masters* by Dr. Brian Weiss. It's about a woman, Catherine (not her real name), who went to Dr. Weiss for help with a fear that had been affecting her life and work. His treatments weren't doing the trick, so he decided to try hypnosis thinking maybe the root of her fear might have been the result of a trauma that had happened to her when she was a baby or toddler—too young to remember. He hypnotized her, and after asking her to go back into her memory, Catherine went into a past life. Here's the interesting part—Catherine was Catholic and didn't believe in past lives. Dr. Weiss is Jewish and doesn't believe in past lives either. But there he was, listening to her detailed accounts of another time and place. In the subsequent sessions, he hypnotized her, and she went back to a few different past lives. And yet, Dr. Weiss remained skeptical, that is until she channeled messages from highly evolved entities who recounted specific details about Dr. Weiss's father and infant son, both of whom had died. There was no way that Catherine herself could have known these personal details, nor could she have somehow researched them.

Catherine talked about the lives her soul had inhabited here on earth, sometimes in a female body and sometimes in a male body. After that particular life had ended, Catherine said that her soul had left that body and had passed from earth to a sort of holding place. It was a place where her soul would rest and contemplate the lesson that she/he needed to learn. Entities whose souls were highly evolved, the "Masters" as they are called in the book, helped guide those resting souls to another spiritual dimension or back to earth to learn another lesson in order for them to progress to higher consciousness levels.

According to not only these Masters, but millions of people throughout the ages who believe in reincarnation, our time here on earth is like school. We learn and go on or fail and repeat a grade. We choose the families we are born into and the challenges that life throws at us.[205] According to those who believe in reincarnation, our souls, who are energy which is neither created nor destroyed, can inhabit bodies on other planets in other galaxies. Those souls or soul groups who have had the experience of being incarnated in another star system often show an interest in both spiritual development and working to make this world a better place.[206]

There have been many who say that *Many Lives, Many Masters* has changed how they view the world—past, present, and future. Others label the book and its premise a shameful hoax. I found it fascinating. I'm not sure I believe in past lives, reincarnation, or spiritual masters, but I know enough to know that I don't know enough. Just imagine the possibilities.

I recently dreamed that I was walking toward the edge of a cliff, as if it were the rim of the earth, and as I inched ever closer, bits of me were breaking off my body and falling to the ground. The sensation was so real that I wrote this poem as soon as I got up.

March 2017

Fantasy

The earth is flat and I am
walking toward the edge.
Suddenly, I am aware that I
have lost my sense of smell. I
continue to walk on when
oops, there goes my hearing. As
I keep walking, I drop pieces of
myself. Oops! Just lost my balance.
Oh well, when I get to the
edge, I'll be a naked little
soul, ready to step over
the edge.

I spoke with Dr. Saravay about my dream and asked what he thought it could mean.

"What do you think is over the edge?" he asked.

"The worst that could happen is nothing—that there's nothing there, and I won't feel a thing. If anything is out there, it has got to be better."

I stood at a bus stop once, and the woman seated beside me looked at me with these sad eyes.

"I'm afraid to grow old," she said to me.

"Think of the alternative."

I myself have never been afraid to grow old. I'm ready to go. The truth is, life isn't as fun anymore. It isn't because I'm lonely, because I like living alone. I like coming home to my apartment where I can do whatever I want whenever I want. I still enjoy going out to lunch and dinner with my family and friends a few times a week. I have a friend, Sarah, come in twice a week to clean the apartment. If I ever felt like I needed extra company, I could always go downstairs in the lobby and talk to people.

Life isn't as fun anymore, because simple chores are hard for me to do now. My eyesight is failing. I lost the sight in my left eye last year, and I've developed a blood clot in my right eye. My doctor, Dr. Shulman, insisted that I won't lose the sight in my right eye, but that I need to be aggressive with the treatments. I'm taking drops three times a day for the swelling in my macula and for glaucoma prevention. I'm also getting an injection in my eyeball every month to dissolve the blood clot. I know what you're thinking. The thought of eyeball injections makes me shudder, too. The clot seems to be breaking up, because my vision is cloudy now. I can't see the paintings on my walls, which is really upsetting. It could take a year for the treatments to work, but my sight will get better. Like the chicken and the egg, I can't help but wonder which will come first—my death or my restored eyesight. Time will tell.

I saw on the news the other day that a woman who is 102 was running a race! NPR ran an article about a French man, Robert Marchand, who is 105 and still setting records on his bicycle. And just look at all that Stephen Hawking did while burdened with his with his ALS. So, I sat myself down and told myself not to worry so much about my eyes. If they could get on with it, so could I.

I'm not afraid to die. I'm curious to know what's beyond the veil, or in my case, what's over the edge of the cliff. There are times when I'd like to stop the train in my reoccurring dream and get off or go back, but then I think about my life and all the things I've seen and done, and I sit back down and let the train move on. Any bend in the road, any different choice made, and I would be different.

What would I change if the choice were mine? Nothing. I've

been blessed beyond measure to have lived such an extraordinary life. I've experienced great pain and even greater joy. I've traveled the world and learned many things about our shared humanity and about myself. I have loved deeply and been loved. Who could ask for more?

After all these years, meeting Auden is the most important and life-altering thing that has happened to me. One of the many things that struck me about that remarkable man was that he listened to me and was honestly interested in what I had to say. I genuinely mattered to him.

"You can be anything you want in this world. You can do anything you want. There's a price on everything. Some people have to pay a lot, and other people get things for bargain prices. But you can do anything you set your mind to."

Throughout my life, Auden's generosity, kindness, and encouragement have never left me. At the end of the movie *Casablanca*, Rick lets Ilsa know that he would always cherish the memory of their brief time together when he said, "We'll always have Paris."

Well, I'll always have Auden.

Gladys Dubovsky in 2017, aged 102

Endnotes

Chapter One

1   Ratzabi, Hila. "What Were Pogroms?" *My Jewish Learning*. http://www.myjewishlearning.com/article/what-were-pogroms/.

2   *The Grossman Project*. "The Pogroms." http://grossmanproject.net/pogroms.htm.

3   Darling, Nancy, Ph.D. "Psychopaths, Children, and Evil." *Psychology Today*. May 14, 2012. https://www.psychologytoday.com/blog/thinking-about-kids/201205/psychopaths-children-and-evil.

Chapter Two

4   Avrich, Paul. *The Modern School Movement: Anarchism and Education in the United States*. (Princeton, NJ: Princeton University Press, 1980), xi.

5   "The Revolution of La Semana Tragica—when Barcelona burned." *Oh-Barcelona: Your trusted host in the city*. August 17, 2017. http://www.oh-barcelona.com/en/blog/things-to-do/history-culture/tragic-week-barcelona-3391.

6   Ibid.

7   "The Stelton Modern School." http://www.talkinghistory.org/stelton/stelton-history.html.

8   Ibid.

9   Avrich, Paul. *The Modern School Movement: Anarchism and Education in the United States*. (Princeton, NJ: Princeton University Press, 1980), xii.

10   "The Stelton Modern School." http://www.talkinghistory.org/stelton/stelton-history.html.

11   Courtney, Steve. "Peekskill's days of infamy." *The Reporter Dispatch*. September 5, 1982. http://www.bencourtney.com/peekskillriots/.

12   Ibid.

13   Salkin, Jeffrey K. "Sixty Years Since the Peekskill Riots." September 2, 2009. http://forward.com/culture/113279/sixty-years-since-the-peekskill-riots/.

14   Ibid.

15   Norris, Michele. "Six Words: 'You've Got To Be Taught' Intolerance." *NPR Morning Edition Special Series collection: the race card project*. May 19, 2014. http://www.npr.org/2014/05/19/308296815/six-words-youve-got-to-be-taught-intolerance.

16   Johnny Simon, Johnny. "The story behind the photo of a screaming white nationalist in Charlottesville." *Quartz*. August 15, 2017. https://qz.com/1054023/charlottesville-torch-photo-white-nationalist-peter-cytanovic-wants-people-to-know-he-is-not-an-evil-nazi/.

Chapter Four

17   Diehl, Lorraine B., Hardart, Marianne. *The Automat: The History, Recipes, and Allure of Horn & Hardart's Masterpiece*. (New York, NY: Clarkson Potter/Publishers a division of Random House, 2002).

Chapter Six

18   "I saw this face, and I fell in love." *The Telegraph*. February 25, 2007. http://www.telegraph.co.uk/culture/books/3663242/I-saw-this-face-and-I-fell-in-love.html.

19   Ibid.

20 "A New Year Greeting" copyright © 1969 from W. H. AUDEN COLLECTED POEMS by W. H. Auden. Used by permission of Random House, an imprint and division of Penguin Random House LLC. All rights reserved.

21 "W.H. Auden." *Poeticous*. https://www.poeticous.com/w-h-auden?al=tff&order=latest&page=4.

22 "W.H. Auden 1907-1973." *Poetry Foundation*. https://www.poetryfoundation.org/poets/w-h-auden.

23 Mendelson, Edward. *Early Auden, Later Auden: A Critical Biography*. (Princeton, NJ: Princeton University Press, 1999), 152.

24 Clark, Thekla. Wystan and Chester: A Personal Memoir of W.H. Auden and Chester Kallman. (New York, NY: Columbia University Press, 1995), 37.

25 Kirsch, Arthur. *Auden and Christianity*. (New Haven, CT: Yale University Press, 2005), 207.

26 Osborne, Charles. *W.H. Auden The Life of a Poet*. (London: The Rainbird Publishing Group Limited, 1979), 106-107.

27 Ibid., 107.

28 Ibid., 120.

29 Helgi Hrafn Guðmundsson, Helgi, Illugadótti, Vera. "The Man Who Didn't Like Hangikjöt: W.H. Auden In Iceland." *The Reykjavík Grapevine*. September 6, 2015. https://grapevine.is/mag/articles/2015/09/06/the-man-who-didnt-like-hangikjot-w-h-auden-in-iceland/.

30 Osborne, Charles. *W.H. Auden The Life of a Poet*. (London: The Rainbird Publishing Group Limited, 1979), 122.

31 Ibid., 109.

32   Martin, David, Mendelson, Edward. "Why Auden Married." *The New York Review of Books.* April 24, 2014. http://www.nybooks.com/articles/2014/04/24/why-auden-married/.

33   Farnan, Dorothy J. *Auden IN LOVE.* (New York, NY.: Simon and Schuster, 1984), 39.

34   Mendelson, Edward. "The Secret Auden." *The New York Review of Books.* March 20, 2014. http://www.nybooks.com/articles/2014/03/20/secret-auden/.

35   Osborne, Charles. *W.H. Auden The Life of a Poet.* (London: The Rainbird Publishing Group Limited, 1979), 225.

36   Ibid.

37   Ibid.

38   "Auden and the churches of Barcelona." *Curlew River.* November 29, 2011. https://curlewriver.wordpress.com/2011/11/29/auden-and-the-churches-of-barcelona/.

39   Huddleston, Robert. "Poetry Makes Nothing Happen, W.H. Auden's Struggle with Politics." *Boston Review.* February 25, 2015. http://bostonreview.net/poetry/robert-huddleston-wh-auden-struggle-politics.

40   Farnan, Dorothy J. *Auden IN LOVE.* (New York, NY.: Simon and Schuster, 1984), 40.

41   "Twelve Songs: XII [Some say that love's a little boy]" copyright © 1940 from W. H. AUDEN COLLECTED POEMS by W. H. Auden. Used by permission of Random House, an imprint and division of Penguin Random House LLC. All rights reserved.

Chapter Seven

42   Carpenter, Humphrey. *W.H. Auden A Biography*, (Boston: Houghton Mifflin Company, 1981), 253.

43   Farnan, Dorothy J. *Auden IN LOVE.* (New York, NY.: Simon and Schuster, 1984), 17-20.

44   Ibid., 23.

45   "Timeline of LGBT history in the United Kingdom." *Wikipedia.* https://en.wikipedia.org/wiki/Timeline_of_LGBT_history_in_the_United_Kingdom.

46   Copeland, Professor Jack. "Alan Turing: The codebreaker who saved 'millions of lives'." *BBC News.* June 19, 2012. http://www.bbc.com/news/technology-18419691.

47   Irving, Clive. "The Castration of Alan Turing, Britain's Code-Breaker WWII Hero." Daily Beast. November 29, 2014. http://www.thedailybeast.com/the-castration-of-alan-turing-britains-code-breaking-wwii-hero.

48   "Lullaby (1937)" copyright © 1940 and renewed 1968 by W. H. Auden, from W. H. AUDEN COLLECTED POEMS by W. H. Auden. Used by permission of Random House, an imprint and division of Penguin Random House LLC. All rights reserved.

49   Kirsch, Arthur. *Auden and Christianity.* (New Haven, CT: Yale University Press, 2005), 207.

50   Tippins, Sherrill. "Genius and High Jinks at 7 Middagh Street." *The New York Times.* February 6, 2005. http://www.nytimes.com/2005/02/06/nyregion/thecity/genius-and-high-jinks-at-7-middagh-street.html.

51   Flood, Alison. "Unseen WH Auden diary sheds light on famous poem and personal life." *The Guardian.* June 26, 2013. https://www.theguardian.com/books/2013/jun/26/auden-diary-bought-british-library.

52   "September 1, 1939" copyright © 1940 and renewed 1968 by W.H. Auden, from W. H. AUDEN COLLECTED POEMS by W. H. Auden. Used by permission of Random House, an imprint and division of Penguin Random House LLC. All rights reserved.

53   Flood, Alison. "Unseen WH Auden diary sheds light on famous poem and personal life." *The Guardian.* June 26, 2013. https://www.theguardian.com/books/2013/jun/26/auden-diary-bought-british-library.

Chapter Eight

54   Osborne, Charles. *W.H. Auden The Life of a Poet.* (London: The Rainbird Publishing Group Limited, 1979), 37.

55   Osbourne, Charles. "W.H. Auden at Oxford." *The New York Times.* October 21, 1979. http://www.nytimes.com/1979/10/21/archives/wh-auden-at-oxford-auden-authors-query.html?_r=0.

56   Fussell, Paul. "The Poet Himself." *The New York Times.* October 4, 1981. http://www.nytimes.com/1981/10/04/books/the-poet-himself.html.

Chapter Nine

57   Zani, Steven. "Blake, William." *Enlightenment Revolution.* November 6, 2008. http://enlightenment-revolution.org/index.php/Blake%2C_William.

58   Livio, Mario. "On William Blake's 'Newton'." HuffPost. October 23, 2014. http://www.huffingtonpost.com/mario-livio/on-william-blakes-newton_b_6036258.html.

59   Essick, Robert N. "Blake in the Marketplace, 2005," *Blake/An Illustrated Quarterly.* Spring 2006, Volume 39, Issue 4. http://bq.blakearchive.org/39.4.essick.

60   "Paradise Lost Book IV." *New Arts Library.* http://www.paradiselost.org/.

Chapter Ten

61   Harrald, Chris, Watkins, Fletcher. The Cigarette Book: The History and Culture of Smoking. (New York, NY: Skyhorse Publishing, 2010), 17.

62   Archambeau. "A Wedding Cake in the Rain: Notes on Auden's Face." *Samizdat Blog.* June 21, 2013. http://samizdatblog.blogspot.com/2013/06/a-wedding-cake-in-rain-notes-on-audens.html.

63   Inglis-Arkell, Esther. "Did Joseph Merrick, known as "elephant man" have Proteus Syndrome?" *io9 We come from the future.* December 18, 2012. http://io9.gizmodo.com/5969314/did-joseph-merrick-known-as-elephant-man-have-proteus-syndrome.

64   Carpenter, Humphrey. *W.H. Auden A Biography*, (Boston: Houghton Mifflin Company, 1981), 275-276.

65   Sacks, Oliver. "Tea at WH Auden's: After work but before the drinking." *Web of Stories.* https://www.webofstories.com/play/oliver.sacks/98;jsessionid=BF6D6DF8A9F52C87F18543A5A4805DD2.

Chapter Eleven

66   "Wagner's Ring Cycle: where to start." *Classic fM Digital Radio.* http://www.classicfm.com/composers/wagner/guides/wagner-ring-cycle-where-start/.

67   Winters, Riley. "The ancient fairy tale of Cupid and Psyche, where love endures against all odds." *Ancient Origins: Reconstructing the Story of Humanity's Past.* July 10, 2015. http://www.ancient-origins.net/myths-legends-europe/ancient-fairy-tale-cupid-and-psyche-where-love-endures-against-all-odds-003393.

68   "The story of Tristan and Isolde." *Ireland Calling: A site dedicated to all things Irish.* http://ireland-calling.com/tristan-and-isolde/.

Chapter Twelve

69   Tippins, Sherrill. "Genius and High Jinks at 7 Middagh Street." *The New York Times.* February 6, 2005. http://www.nytimes.com/2005/02/06/nyregion/thecity/genius-and-high-jinks-at-7-middagh-street.html.

70   Ibid.

71   Carpenter, Humphrey. *W.H. Auden A Biography*, (Boston: Houghton Mifflin Company, 1981), 304.

72   Farnan, Dorothy J. *Auden IN LOVE.* (New York, NY.: Simon and Schuster, 1984), 28.

73   Jenkins, Nicholas. "Jack Barker: 1915-1995." *The W. H. Auden Society.* April 1996. http://audensociety.org/14newsletter.html.

74   Ibid.

75   Farnan, Dorothy J. *Auden IN LOVE.* (New York, NY.: Simon and Schuster, 1984), 55-56.

76   Ibid.

77   Ibid., 56-57.

78   Jenkins, Nicholas. "Jack Barker: 1915-1995." *The W. H. Auden Society*. April 1996. http://audensociety.org/14newsletter.html.

79   Mitchel, Duncan. "Small, But Most Sympathetic." *This Is So Gay*. December 26, 2007.
http://thisislikesogay.blogspot.com/2007/12/small-but-most-sympathetic.html.

80   Carpenter, Humphrey. *W.H. Auden A Biography*, (Boston: Houghton Mifflin Company, 1981), 316.

81   Miranda Seymour, Miranda. "The Woman in Their Lives." *The New York Times*. September 22, 1996. http://www.nytimes.com/1996/09/22/books/the-woman-in-their-lives.html.

82   Hekma, Gert. "An Extraordinary Experiment In Communal Living in Brooklyn." *Gay News*. June 12, 2005. http://www.gay-news.com/article/1173/7---An-Extraordinary-Experiment-In-Communal-Living-in-Brooklyn/.

83   Carpenter, Humphrey. *W.H. Auden A Biography*, (Boston: Houghton Mifflin Company, 1981), 313.

84   Haven, Cynthia. "Song without music: Auden's 'For the Time Being: A Christmas Oratorio." *Stanford University: The Book Haven Cynthia Haven's Blog for the Written Word*. December 23, 2014. http://bookhaven.stanford.edu/tag/chester-kallman/.

85   Farnan, Dorothy J. *Auden IN LOVE*. (New York, NY.: Simon and Schuster, 1984), 65.

86   Tippins, Sherill. February House: *The Story of W.H. Auden, Carson McCullers, Jane and Paul Bowles, Benjamin Britten, and Gypsy Rose Lee, Under One Roof in Brooklyn*. (Boston, MA.: Houghton Mifflin Harcourt, 2005), 244.

87   Farnan, Dorothy J. "Christmas Day. 1941." *Auden IN LOVE*. (New York, NY.: Simon and Schuster, 1984), 67. Permission granted by Edward Mendelson.

Literary Executor of the Estate of W. H. Auden. The poem is copyright by the Estate of W. H. Auden.

Chapter Thirteen

88   Farnan, Dorothy J. *Auden IN LOVE.* (New York, NY.: Simon and Schuster, 1984), 67.

89   Ibid.

90   Tippins, Sherill. February House: *The Story of W.H. Auden, Carson McCullers, Jane and Paul Bowles, Benjamin Britten, and Gypsy Rose Lee, Under One Roof in Brooklyn.* (Boston, MA.: Houghton Mifflin Harcourt, 2005), 244.

91   Auden, W.H., Bucknell, Katherine. *"In Solitude, for Company": W. H. Auden after 1940: Unpublished Prose and Recent Criticism.* (Gloucestershire, United Kingdom: Clarendon Press-Oxford University Press, 1995), 12.

92   Ibid., 78.

93   Ibid., 78-79.

94   Ibid., 79-80.

Chapter Fourteen

95   McCall Smith, Alexander. "What W.H. Auden can teach us in times of crisis," *Financial Times.* March 14, 2014. https://www.ft.com/content/6a5450ac-a90b-11e3-bf0c-00144feab7de.

96   Tippins, Sherill. "A literary oasis in 1940s Brooklyn." The New York Times. February 9, 2005. http://www.nytimes.com/2005/02/09/arts/a-literary-oasis-in-1940s-brooklyn.html.

97 "Timeline of World War II: 1943." *Learn NC UNC School of Education.* http://www.learnnc.org/lp/table.php?id=5972.

98 Clifford Larson, Kate. *Rosemary: The Hidden Kennedy Daughter*, (New York: Houghton Mifflin Harcourt Publishing Company, 2015), 3.

99 Lenz, Lyz. "The Secret Lobotomy of Rosemary Kennedy." *Marie Claire.* March 31, 2017. http://www.marieclaire.com/celebrity/a26261/secret-loboto-my-rosemary-kennedy/.

100 Shapiro, Joseph. "Eunice Kennedy Shriver's Olympic Legacy." *NPR Morning Edition.* April 5, 2007. https://www.npr.org/templates/story/story.php?story-Id=9136962.

Chapter Fifteen

101 "The United States and the Holocaust." Holocaust Encyclopedia. https://www.ushmm.org/wlc/en/article.php?ModuleId=10005182.

102 Loudon, Irvine. *The Tragedy of Childbed Fever*, (Oxford, United Kingdom: Oxford University Press, 2000), 5-6.

103 Burch, Druin. "When Childbirth Was Natural, and Deadly." *Live Science.* January 10, 2009. https://www.livescience.com/3210-childbirth-natural-deadly.html.

Chapter Sixteen

104 "Liberation of Nazi Camps." *Holocaust Encyclopedia.* https://www.ushmm.org/wlc/en/article.php?ModuleId=10005131.

105 Glass, Andrew. "President Franklin D. Roosevelt dies at ag 63, April 12, 1945." *Politico.* April 12, 2016. https://www.politico.com/story/2016/04/this-day-in-politics-april-12-1945-221722.

106 "1945 FDR dies." *History: April 12 This Day In History.* http://www.history.com/this-day-in-history/fdr-dies.

107 Klein, Christopher. "Mussolini's Final Hours, 70 Years Ago." *History: History Stories.* April 28, 2015. http://www.history.com/news/mussolinis-final-hours-70-years-ago.

108 "Eva Braun: The Suicide," http://www.evabraun.dk/evabraun4.htm.

109 "President Harry S. Truman reads prepared speech after dropping of atomic bomb on ...HD Stock Footage." *YouTube CriticalPast.* April 8, 2014. https://www.youtube.com/watch?v=e3Ib4wTq0jY.

110 Price, Greg. "Trump's North Korea Threat is Eerily Similar to Harry Truman's Hiroshima Bombing Announcement in 1945." *Newsweek.* August 8, 2017. http://www.newsweek.com/trump-north-korea-threat-truman-hiroshima-648304.

111 McIntyre, Jamie. "US commander didn't ask permission to drop 'the Mother of All Bombs'." *Washington Examiner.* April 14, 2017. http://www.washingtonexaminer.com/us-commander-didnt-ask-permission-to-drop-the-mother-of-all-bombs/article/2620309.

112 Lovinger, Paul W., Scott, Harry. "Why Bush's War Is Illegal." *War and Law League (WALL).* http://www.warandlaw.org/files/bushwar.htm.

113 E, Ernest. "Televangelist Jim Bakker Says Christians Will Start A Civil War If Trump Is Impeached." *Democratic Moms.* August 30, 2017. http://democraticmoms.com/televangelist-jim-bakker-says-christians-will-start-a-civil-war-if-trump-is-impeached/.

Chapter Seventeen

114 Costello, Bonnie, Galvin, Rachel. *Auden at Work.* (London, United Kingdom: Palgrave MacMillan, August 2015), 260-270.

115 Brockman, Stephen. "Nuremberg: The Imaginary Capital." (Rochester, NY: Camden House, 2006), 222-223.

116 Osborne, Charles. *W.H. Auden The Life of a Poet.* (London: The Rainbird Publishing Group Limited, 1979), 220.

117 Flood, Alison. "Unseen WH Auden diary sheds light on famous poem and personal life." The Guardian. June 26, 2013. https://www.theguardian.com/books/2013/jun/26/auden-diary-bought-british-library.

118 Osborne, Charles. *W.H. Auden The Life of a Poet.* (London: The Rainbird Publishing Group Limited, 1979), 221.

119 Ibid., 225.

120 "Anonymous, Chester Kallman in Drag, 1945." Permission granted by Guy Berube, Director, LPM Projects, Ottawa, Canada.

Chapter Eighteen

121 Lewis, Victoria. "The History of Department Store Holiday Window Displays." *Zady.* https://zady-com1.a.ssl.fastly.net/features/the-history-of-department-store-holiday-window-displays.

122 "First Victorian Christmas Tree." *Victorian Magazine.* http://www.victoriana.com/christmas/tree-99.htm.

Chapter Nineteen

123 Osborne, Charles. *W.H. Auden The Life of a Poet.* (London: The Rainbird Publishing Group Limited, 1979), 226.

124 Ibid., 227-228.

125 "Ischia" from W. H. AUDEN COLLECTED POEMS by W. H. Auden, copyright © 1976 by Edward Mendelson, William Meredith and Monroe K. Spears, Executors of the Estate of W.H. Auden. Used by permission of Random House, an imprint and division of Penguin Random House LLC. All rights reserved.

126 Allen, Liam. "Defection probe over poet Auden." *BBC News*. March 2, 2007. http://news.bbc.co.uk/2/hi/uk_news/6407793.stm.

127 Osborne, Charles. *W.H. Auden The Life of a Poet*. (London: The Rainbird Publishing Group Limited, 1979), 237.

128 Clark, Thekla. Wystan and Chester: A Personal Memoir of W.H. Auden and Chester Kallman. (New York, NY: Columbia University Press, 1995), 10.

129 Ibid., 31.

130 Ibid., 20-21.

131 Carpenter, Humphrey. *W.H. Auden A Biography*, (Boston: Houghton Mifflin Company, 1981), 371.

132 "W.H. Auden: An English poet in the East Village." *Ephemeral New York*. October 24, 2008. https://ephemeralnewyork.wordpress.com/2008/10/24/wh-auden-an-english-poet-in-the-east-village/.

133 Loew, Karen. "Happy Birthday W.H. Auden, East Villager." *Off the Grid: The Blog of Greenwich Village Society for Historic Preservation*. February 21, 2014. http://gvshp.org/blog/2014/02/21/happy-birthday-w-h-auden-east-villager/.
134 "W.H. Auden." Poeticous. https://www.poeticous.com/w-h-auden?al=tff&order=latest&page=4.

135 Calhoun, Ada. *St. Mark's Is Dead: The Many Lives of America's Hippest Street*. (New York, NY: W.W. Norton & Co., 2015 1ˢᵗ Edition), 275.

Chapter Twenty

136 Diament, Michelle. "Obama Signs Bill Replacing 'Mental Retardation' With 'Intellectual Disability.'" disabilityscoop: The Premier Source for Developmental Disability News. October 5, 2010. https://www.disabilityscoop.com/2010/10/05/obama-signs-rosas-law/10547/.

137 Osborne, Charles. *W.H. Auden The Life of a Poet.* (London: The Rainbird Publishing Group Limited, 1979), 247.

138 Clark, Thekla. Wystan and Chester: A Personal Memoir of W.H. Auden and Chester Kallman. (New York, NY: Columbia University Press, 1995), 25-26.

139 Ibid., 41.

140 "In Memoriam L.K.-A. 1950-1952" from W. H. AUDEN COLLECTED POEMS by W. H. Auden, copyright © 1976 by Edward Mendelson, William Meredith and Monroe K. Spears, Executors of the Estate of W.H. Auden. Used by permission of Random House, an imprint and division of Penguin Random House LLC. All rights reserved.

141 Osborne, Charles. *W.H. Auden The Life of a Poet.* (London: The Rainbird Publishing Group Limited, 1979), 247.

Chapter Twenty-One

142 Morton, Frederic. "Letter From Vienna." *The New York Times.* May 7, 1978. http://www.nytimes.com/1978/05/07/archives/letter-from-vienna-vienna.html?_r=0.
143 Osborne, Charles. *W.H. Auden The Life of a Poet.* (London: The Rainbird Publishing Group Limited, 1979), 248.

144 W.H. Auden. *Poeticous.* https://www.poeticous.com/w-h-auden?al=tff&order=latest&page=4.

145 Clark, Thekla. Wystan and Chester: A Personal Memoir of W.H. Auden and Chester Kallman. (New York, NY: Columbia University Press, 1995), 41.

146 Ibid.

147 Ibid., 63.

Chapter Twenty-Two

148 DeNoon, Daniel, J. "Dry Cleaning Chemical 'Likely' Causes Cancer." *WebMD*. February 9, 2010. https://www.webmd.com/cancer/news/20100209/dry-cleaning-chemical-likely-causes-cancer#1.

149 Osborne, Charles. *W.H. Auden The Life of a Poet*. (London: The Rainbird Publishing Group Limited, 1979), 254.

150 "Elegy for J.F.K." copyright © 1965 by W.H. Auden, from W. H. AUDEN COLLECTED POEMS by W. H. Auden. Used by permission of Random House, an imprint and division of Penguin Random House LLC. All rights reserved.

151 Osborne, Charles. *W.H. Auden The Life of a Poet*. (London: The Rainbird Publishing Group Limited, 1979), 278-279.

152 "The Vietnam Lotteries." *Selective Service System*. https://www.sss.gov/About/History-And-Records/lotter1.

153 Califano, Joseph, A. "Seeing Is Believing - The Enduring Legacy of Lyndon Johnson." *LBJ Presidential Library*. May 19, 2008. http://www.lbjlibrary.org/lyndon-baines-johnson/perspectives-and-essays/seeing-is-believing-the-enduring-legacy-of-lyndon-johnson.

Chapter Twenty-Three

154 Cowell, Alan, Gladstone, Rick. "Do Spy Agencies Hold Answers to Dag Hammarskjold's Death? U.N. Wants to Know." The New York Times. July 15, 2017.

https://www.nytimes.com/2017/07/15/world/africa/dag-hammarskjold-united-na-tions-mohamed-chande-othman.html.

155 Mendelson, Edward. "The Secret Auden." *The New York Review of Books*. March 20, 2014. http://www.nybooks.com/articles/2014/03/20/secret-auden/.

156 "The Cave of Making" copyright © 1964 from W. H. AUDEN COLLECTED POEMS by W. H. Auden. Used by permission of Random House, an imprint and division of Penguin Random House LLC. All rights reserved.

157 G., Alexandra. "Why was Archduke Franz Ferdinand Assassinated and how was this a catalyst for WWI?" *MyTutor*. https://www.mytutor.co.uk/answers/9170/GCSE/History/Why-was-Archduke-Franz-Ferdinand-Assassinated-and-how-was-this-a-catalyst-for-WW1.

158 "This Day In History: 1914 Archduke Franz Ferdinand assassinated." *History*. http://www.history.com/this-day-in-history/archduke-franz-ferdinand-assassinated.

Chapter Twenty-Four

159 Osborne, Charles. *W.H. Auden The Life of a Poet*. (London: The Rainbird Publishing Group Limited, 1979), 256.

160 Ibid., 288.

161 Carpenter, Humphrey. *W.H. Auden A Biography*, (Boston: Houghton Mifflin Company, 1981), 427.

162 Osborne, Charles. *W.H. Auden The Life of a Poet*. (London: The Rainbird Publishing Group Limited, 1979), 290-291.

163 Ibid., 431.

164 "Old People's Home" copyright © 1970 from W. H. AUDEN COLLECT-ED POEMS by W. H. Auden. Used by permission of Random House, an imprint and division of Penguin Random House LLC. All rights reserved.

165 Carpenter, Humphrey. *W.H. Auden A Biography*, (Boston: Houghton Mifflin Company, 1981), 430.

166 Ibid., 432.

Chapter Twenty-Five

167 Simon Rodberg, "The CIO without the CIA," http://prospect.org/article/cio-without-cia. (December 19, 2001).

168 Walsh, John. "Auden: The lost poems." *Independent*. September 4, 2007. http://www.independent.co.uk/arts-entertainment/books/features/auden-the-lost-poems-463874.html.

169 "[He still loves life]" from THANK YOU, FOG by W. H. Auden, copyright © 1972, 1973 by W. H. Auden. Copyright © 1973, 1974 by the Estate of W. H. Auden. Used by permission of Random House, an imprint and division of Penguin Random House LLC. All rights reserved.

170 Shenker, Israel. "W.H. Auden Dies in Vienna." *The New York Times*. September 30, 1973. http://www.nytimes.com/1973/09/30/archives/w-h-auden-dies-in-vienna-w-h-auden-dies-in-vienna-at-the-age-of-66.html.

171 Osborne, Charles. *W.H. Auden The Life of a Poet*. (London: The Rainbird Publishing Group Limited, 1979), 294-295.

172 Ibid., 296.

173 Carpenter, Humphrey. *W.H. Auden A Biography*, (Boston: Houghton Mifflin Company, 1981), 439.

174 Osborne, Charles. *W.H. Auden The Life of a Poet*. (London: The Rainbird Publishing Group Limited, 1979), 298.

Chapter Twenty-Six

175 Popova, Maria. "The Art of Medicine: W.H. Auden on What Makes a Great Physician and How He Influenced Oliver Sacks." Brain Pickings. https://www. brainpickings.org/2016/05/19/w-h-auden-commonplace-book-medicine/.

176 "The poem that W.H. Auden dedicated to Oliver Sacks." *Tribrach: for those who love (or would like to love) poetry*. January 6, 2016. https://tribrach.wordpress. com/2016/01/09/the-poem-that-w-h-auden-dedicated-to-oliver-sacks/.

177 Popova, Maria. "The Art of Medicine: W.H. Auden on What Makes a Great Physician and How He Influenced Oliver Sacks." Brain Pickings. https://www. brainpickings.org/2016/05/19/w-h-auden-commonplace-book-medicine/.

178 "The poem that W.H. Auden dedicated to Oliver Sacks." *Tribrach: for those who love (or would like to love) poetry*. January 6, 2016. https://tribrach.wordpress. com/2016/01/09/the-poem-that-w-h-auden-dedicated-to-oliver-sacks/.

179 Silberman, Steve. "The Fully Immersive Mind of Oliver Sacks." *Wired*. April, 1, 2002. https://www.wired.com/2002/04/sacks-2/.

Chapter Twenty-Seven

180 Silberman, Steve. "The Fully Immersive Mind of Oliver Sacks." *Wired*. April, 1, 2002. https://www.wired.com/2002/04/sacks-2/.

181 Farnan, Dorothy J. *Auden IN LOVE*. (New York, NY.: Simon and Schuster, 1984), 13-14.

182 Osborne, Charles. *W.H. Auden The Life of a Poet*. (London: The Rainbird Publishing Group Limited, 1979), 306.

183 "I saw this face, and I fell in love." *The Telegraph*. February 25, 2007. http://www.telegraph.co.uk/culture/books/3663242/I-saw-this-face-and-I-fell-in-love.html.

184 Osborne, Charles. *W.H. Auden The Life of a Poet*. (London: The Rainbird Publishing Group Limited, 1979), 307.

185 Ibid., 308.

186 Morton, Frederic. "Letter From Vienna." *The New York Times*. May 7, 1978. http://www.nytimes.com/1978/05/07/archives/letter-from-vienna-vienna.html?_r=0.

187 Carpenter, Humphrey. *W.H. Auden A Biography*, (Boston: Houghton Mifflin Company, 1981), 452.

188 Osborne, Charles. *W.H. Auden The Life of a Poet*. (London: The Rainbird Publishing Group Limited, 1979), 310.

189 Carpenter, Humphrey. *W.H. Auden A Biography*. (Boston: Houghton Mifflin Company, 1981), 453.

190 Jackson, David. "Kallman in Athens." *The New York Review of Books*. October 25, 1984. http://www.nybooks.com/articles/1984/10/25/kallman-in-athens-1/.
191 Pugetopolis. "When Chester Kallman died." Arielesque. November 25, 2010. http://arielesque.blogspot.com/2010/11/when-chester-kallman-died.html.

192 "Funeral Blues" copyright © 1940 and renewed 1968 by W. H. Auden, from W. H. AUDEN COLLECTED POEMS by W. H. Auden. Used by permission of Random House, an imprint and division of Penguin Random House LLC. All rights reserved.

Chapter Twenty-Eight

193 "The poem that W.H. Auden dedicated to Oliver Sacks." *Tribrach: for those who love (or would like to love) poetry*. January 6, 2016. https://tribrach.wordpress.com/2016/01/09/the-poem-that-w-h-auden-dedicated-to-oliver-sacks/.

194 "Leonardo Da Vinci—An Artist and a Military Engineer." Ocher Art. June 9, 2016. https://ocherart.wordpress.com/tag/da-vincis-flying-machine/.

195 Jones, Jonathan. "How Leonardo da Vinci's angels pointed the way to the future." *The Guardian*. December 24, 2012. https://www.theguardian.com/artand-design/jonathanjonesblog/2012/dec/25/leonardo-da-vinci-angels-flying-machine.

196 "Activity: Mirror Writing." Museum of Science. https://www.mos.org/leonardo/activities/mirror-writing.

Chapter Twenty-Nine

197 Levy, Alan. *W.H. Auden: In the Autumn of the Age of Anxiety*. (Sag Harbor, NY: The Permanent Press, 1983).

Chapter Thirty

198 "Sudden Cardiac Death (Sudden Cardiac Arrest)." *Cleveland Clinic*. March 3, 2017. https://my.clevelandclinic.org/health/articles/sudden-cardiac-death.

Chapter Thirty-One

199 Lubasch, Arnold H. "Shot by Shot, an Ex-Aide to Gotti Describes the Killing of Castellano." The New York Times. March 4, 1992. http://www.nytimes.com/1992/03/04/nyregion/shot-by-shot-an-ex-aide-to-gotti-describes-the-killing-of-castellano.html?pagewanted=all.

200 Editors of the New York Daily News. "The day Paul Castellano was assassinated outside Sparks Steak House in notorious mob hit." New York Daily News. December 15, 2014. http://www.nydailynews.com/new-york/archives-big-paul-chauffeur-ride-article-1.2043547.

201 Bilyeau, Nancy. "Why ordering a hit on "big Paul" Castellano at Sparks Steak House was John Gotti's big mistake. The Vintage News. August 8, 2017. https://www.thevintagenews.com/2017/08/08/why-ordering-a-hit-on-big-paul-castellano-at-sparks-steak-house-was-john-gottis-big-mistake/.

Chapter Thirty-Two

202 Christie, Joel, Maysh, Jeff. "The 'dust lady' of 9/11 dies: Iconic survivor Marcy Borders, 42, succumbs to stomach cancer which she blamed on ash from the Twin Towers attack." *Daily Mail*. August 25, 2015. http://www.dailymail.co.uk/news/article-3211020/The-dusty-lady-9-11-Marcy-Borders-dies-stomach-cancer-ash-Twin-Towers-decade-long-battle-depression.html.

203 "September 1, 1939" copyright © 1940 and renewed 1968 by W.H. Auden, from W. H. AUDEN COLLECTED POEMS by W. H. Auden. Used by permission of Random House, an imprint and division of Penguin Random House LLC. All rights reserved.

Chapter Thirty-Five

204 Wikipedia, "Dudley Moore," https://en.wikipedia.org/wiki/Dudley_Moore.

205 "Chapter 5. Reincarnation." *Afterlife 101*. 2002. http://www.afterlife101.com/Chapter5.html#_Toc1998622.

206 Guru, Grace. "Do Our Souls Come From A Different Planet Or Universe?" August 15, 2015. http://graceguru.net/do-our-souls-come-from-a-different-planet-or-universe/.

About the Author

Debbie has an MFA in creative writing from Florida International University. She has written two other books: *A Crowded Loneliness: The story of loss, survival and resilience of a Peter Pan Child of Cuba* and *The Fisherman*, a novel set during the Prohibition. She lives in Upstate New York.

www.debbieshannon.com

CPSIA information can be obtained
at www.ICGtesting.com
Printed in the USA
FFHW011955281118
49693583-54088FF

9 781948 981125